The Cluetrain Manifesto

The Cluetrain Manifesto

The end of business as usual

RICK LEVINE

CHRISTOPHER LOCKE

DOC SEARLS

DAVID WEINBERGER

An imprint of Pearson Education

London · New York · San Francisco · Toronto · Sydney · Tokyo · Singapore
Hong Kong · Cape Town · Madrid · Amsterdam · Munich · Paris · Milan

PEARSON EDUCATION LIMITED

Head Office
Edinburgh Gate
Harlow CM20 2JE
Tel: +44 (0)1279 623623
Fax: +44 (0)1279 431059

London Office:
128 Long Acre
London WC2E 9AN
Tel: +44 (0)20 7447 2000
Fax: +44 (0)20 7240 5771
Website:www.business-minds.com

_____

First published in the United States in 2000 by Perseus Publishing,
a subsidiary of Perseus Books L.L.C.

First published in Great Britain in 2000

© Frederick Levine, Christopher Locke, David Searls, and David Weinberger 2000

ISBN 0 273 65023 8

British Library Cataloguing in Publication Data
A CIP catalogue record for this book can be obtained from the British Library.

10 9 8 7 6 5 4 3 2 1

Typeset by Northern Phototypesetting Co. Ltd, Bolton
Printed and bound in Great Britain by Biddles Ltd, Guildford & King's Lynn

The Publishers' policy is to use paper manufactured from sustainable forests.

CONTENTS

Ancient markets were full of the sound of life: conversation. They dealt in craft goods that bore the marks of the people who made them. Then mass production led to mass marketing and mass media: interchangeable workers, products and consumers, along with the hierarchical bureaucracies needed to command and control them. But the Internet – unmanaged and full of the sound of the human voice – is proving that the Industrial Age is nothing but an interruption as the conversations resume, this time on a global scale.

Our culture has greeted the Web with such enthusiasm, even before we've understood what exactly it's for, because we believe it's returning something we miss deeply: our voices. We are now ending the Faustian bargain according to which we gave up much of our individuality at work in return for the illusion of living in a manageable, safe world. as we emerge into the new understanding, it is being revealed that this cultural change is in fact spiritual

Voice – the authentic expression of the individual present in the craft-work of our hands as well as in our words – is in resurgence on the Internet. In fact, the Internet is a conversation carried on in a variety of formats – Web pages, e-mail, discussion groups, mailing lists – that bring new possibilities to human relations. Business-as-usual isn't happy about this, because conversations are unpredictable, messy and uncontrollable. But there's no silencing our human voices. Wise companies will learn how to enter the conversation.

The mass production of the industrial world led companies to engage in mass marketing, delivery 'messages' to undifferentiated hordes who didn't want to receive them. Now the Web is enabling the market to converse again, as people tell one another the truth about products and companies and their own desires – learning faster than business. Companies have to figure out how to enter this global conversation rather than relying on the old marketing techniques of public relations, marketing communications, advertising and other forms of propaganda. We, the market, don't want messages at all, we want to speak with your business in a human voice.

Like their counterparts in the marketplace, intranetworked employees are learning to speak in their own voice, ignoring the organisation charts and telling the truth to one another – and to their customers. The direct connection, worker to worker, enabled by intranets is undermining the old management pyramid, turning the walls of Fort Business into conversations. From the bottom up, businesses are beginning to accept openness, decentralisation, fallibility, messy context-rich information stories and the sound of the authentic voices of individuals.

We're living through a change of historic proportions, so there are no easy
answers. In fact, there aren't even an easy questions any more. the ones most
commonly asked – in magazine articles and political speeches – are disguised
attempts to distract us from the truly deep changes that are coccurring. We'd
do far better to learn to listen to the questions coming from our hearts.

The only revolution that matters is already well under way and by the way,
we're winning). A strange and oddly playful attitude is in evidence nearly
everywhere online, an ironic shared intelligence that subverts the core
assumptions of traditional institutions. There's fun afoot on the Internet, and
business had better take it seriously. When paradox becomes paradigm, it's
already too late to look for a magic-bullet cure for Corporate Linguistic Deficit
Disorder. It's time to imagine entirely new roles, new reasons, new worlds.

FOREWORD

TAKE A POT OF WATER that's just above the freezing mark. Now, crank up the heat and wait. Temperature rises. Wait some more. Go all the way to 211 degrees Fahrenheit and nothing looks much different. But then, turn it up one more tiny degree, and wham! The pot becomes a roiling, steamy cauldron.

Don't look now, but you're holding such a catalyst in your hands. *The Cluetrain Manifesto* is about to drive business to a full boil.

Let me tell you how it took me to the tipping point. Not long ago I was sitting in the Hotel Nikko in San Francisco on a reporting mission for 'The Front Lines', a weekly column I spent four years writing for *The Wall Street Journal*. Between interviews, I was checking e-mail from my readers. (The Internet puts me in touch with thousands of them who act as my scouts.) On this particular day, one of my correspondents urged me to check out a new site at www.cluetrain.com.

I was dumbstruck. There, in a few pages, I read a startlingly concise summary of everything I'd seen in 21 years as a reporter, editor, bureau chief and columnist for my newspaper. The idea that business, at the core, is fundamentally human. That engineering remains second-rate without aesthetics. That natural, human conversation is the true language of commerce. That corporations work best when the people on the inside have the fullest contact possible with the people on the outside.

And most importantly, that however ancient, timeless and true, these principles are just now resurging across the business world. The triggering event, of course, is the advent of a global communication system that restores the banter of the bazaar, that tears down power structures and senseless bureaucracies, that puts everyone in touch with everyone.

Scrolling through the hundreds of signatories who had endorsed the manifesto, I realised this if nothing else: The newspaper gods had just blessed me with one of my favourite columns ever, enabling me to articulate much I knew to be true but never previously had the words to say.

Because 'The Front Lines' was usually a narrative tale, I bored into the manifesto's origins. Befitting its message, the document, I learned, was born in an extended electronic conversation among four Internet denizens spread from coast to coast. The authors were not the ultra-hip, just-outta-college webheads I had imagined. One was Rick Levine, a Boulder-based engineer for the giant Sun Microsystems. Another was a Boulder consultant named Christopher Locke, late of such hoary outfits as IBM, MCI and Carnegie Mellon. There was a well-known Silicon Valley publicist named Doc Searls and a longtime high-tech marketer from Boston whose name, David Weinberger, I recognised from his commentaries on National Public Radio's 'All Things Considered'.

They were, in short, fixtures of the high-tech establishment – but being establishment made their renunciation of business-as-usual all the more powerful.

The manifesto URL leaped between cubicles like mononucleosis through a co-ed dorm. Some readers found it pretentious, bordering on smug. (To those of delicate sensibility, it was.) Some found it nihilistic. (It wasn't.) But all found it arresting and impossible to ignore. The manifesto became a kind of user's guide to the Internet economy – a world of new online communities; of self-organising corporate employees; of Linux and other 'open source' movements that seem to erupt from thin air.

So now, for anyone who missed it the first time and for everyone else who wants more, we have *The Cluetrain Manifesto*, one of the first books written as a sequel to a Web site.

I look at a huge number of business books. I actually read some of them and have published reviews on more than my share. I'll mention a few ways *The Cluetrain Manifesto* is like no other.

First, this is no feel-good book. Though the broad theme is overwhelmingly optimistic, the details will make you squirm. This is an obituary for business-as-usual. It shows how your Web strategy may be minutes from obsolescence. It reveals how the Internet has made your entry-level employees as powerful as your senior vice-president of marketing. Recall what *The Jungle* did to meat packing, what *Silent Spring* did to chemicals, what *Unsafe at any Speed* did to Detroit. That's the spirit with which *The Cluetrain Manifesto* takes on the arrogance of corporate e-commerce. (Notably, some of the best material comes from the authors' own experiences within big companies, and they name names.)

Second, this is not a how-to book, unless you need a remedial lesson in being human. For all their righteous self-assuredness about the Internet revolution, these authors don't presume to tell you how to run your business or your career. One-size-fits-all 'programmes' and 'methodologies' are just ways for consultants to gouge clients and book buyers. Instead, this book simply describes business *as it really is* and *as it's really becoming*. You'll come away from these pages with a new set of eyes for redirecting your career or rehabilitating your company according to its own unique circumstances.

Third, this book is not boring. The whole message here, after all, involves speaking with a human voice. That means stories instead of lectures, humour instead of hubris, description instead of PowerPoint pie charts. (Imagine *In Search of Excellence* crossed with *Fear and Loathing in Las Vegas*.) When was the last time you laughed out loud reading a business book?

And why not laughter? It's one of the signature tunes of human conversation. This book shows how conversation forms the basis of business, how business lost that voice for a while, and how that language is returning to business thanks to a technology that inspires, and in many cases demands, that we speak from the heart.

To rip off what rock critic Jon Landau once said about Bruce Springsteen: I've seen the future of business, and it's *The Cluetrain Manifesto*.

At first you may be tempted to hide this book inside the dust jacket for *Customers.com* or something equally conventional. But in time you'll see the book spreading. It will become acceptable, if never entirely accepted. It will certainly become essential. Why am I so sure? Because like nothing else out there, it shows us how to grasp the human side of business and technology, and being human, try as we might, is the only fate from which we can never escape.

–Thomas Petzinger, Jr
The Wall Street Journal

THE CLUETRAIN MANIFESTO

People of Earth ...

A POWERFUL GLOBAL CONVERSATION has begun. Through the Internet, people are discovering and inventing new ways to share relevant knowledge with blinding speed. As a direct result, markets are getting smarter – and getting smarter faster than most companies.

These markets are conversations. Their members communicate in language that is natural, open, honest, direct, funny, and often shocking. Whether explaining or complaining, joking or serious, the human voice is unmistakably genuine. It can't be faked.

Most corporations, on the other hand, only know how to talk in the soothing, humourless monotone of the mission statement, marketing brochure and your-call-is-important-to-us busy signal. Same old tone, same old lies. No wonder networked markets have no respect for companies unable or unwilling to speak as they do.

But learning to speak in a human voice is not some trick, nor will corporations convince us they are human with lip service about 'listening to customers'. They will only sound human when they empower real human beings to speak on their behalf.

While many such people already work for companies today, most companies ignore their ability to deliver genuine knowledge, opting instead to crank out sterile happytalk that insults the intelligence of markets literally too smart to buy it.

However, employees are getting hyperlinked even as markets are. Companies need to listen carefully to both. Mostly, they need to get out of the way so intranetworked employees can converse directly with internetworked markets.

Corporate firewalls have kept smart employees in and smart markets out. It's going to cause real pain to tear those walls down. But the result will be a new kind of conversation. And it will be the most exciting conversation business has ever engaged in.

95 Theses

1   Markets are conversations.

2   Markets consist of human beings, not demographic sectors.

3   Conversations among human beings *sound* human. They are conducted in a human voice.

4   Whether delivering information, opinions, perspectives, dissenting arguments or humorous asides, the human voice is typically open, natural, uncontrived.

5   People recognise each other as such from the sound of this voice.

6   The Internet is enabling conversations among human beings that were simply not possible in the era of mass media.

7   Hyperlinks subvert hierarchy.

8   In both *inter*networked markets and among *intra*networked employees, people are speaking to each other in a powerful new way.

9   These networked conversations are enabling powerful new forms of social organisation and knowledge exchange to emerge.

10   As a result, markets are getting smarter, more informed, more organised. Participation in a networked market changes people fundamentally.

11   People in networked markets have figured out that they get far better information and support from one another than from vendors. So much for corporate rhetoric about adding value to commoditised products.

12   There are no secrets. The networked market knows more than companies do about their own products. And whether the news is good or bad, they tell everyone.

13   What's happening to markets is also happening among employees. A metaphysical construct called 'The Company' is the only thing standing between the two.

14   Corporations do not speak in the same voice as these new networked conversations. To their intended online audiences, companies sound hollow, flat, literally inhuman.

15   In just a few more years, the current homogenised 'voice' of business – the sound of mission statements and brochures – will seem as contrived and artificial as the language of the 18th-century French court.

16   Already, companies that speak in the language of the pitch, the dog-and-pony show, are no longer speaking to anyone.

17   Companies that assume online markets are the same markets that used to watch their ads on television are kidding themselves.

18   Companies that don't realise their markets are now networked person-to-person, getting smarter as a result and deeply joined in conversation are missing their best opportunity.

19   Companies can now communicate with their markets directly. If they blow it, it could be their last chance.

20   Companies need to realise their markets are often laughing. At them.

21   Companies need to lighten up and take themselves less seriously. They need to get a sense of humour.

22   Getting a sense of humour does not mean putting some jokes on the corporate Web site. Rather, it requires big values, a little humility, straight talk and a genuine point of view.

23   Companies attempting to 'position' themselves need to *take* a position. Optimally, it should relate to something their market actually cares about.

24   Bombastic boasts – 'We are positioned to become the pre-eminent provider of XYZ' – do not constitute a position.

25   Companies need to come down from their Ivory Towers and talk to the people with whom they hope to create relationships.

26   Public Relations does not relate to the public. Companies are deeply afraid of their markets.

27   By speaking in language that is distant, uninviting, arrogant, they build walls to keep markets at bay.

28   Most marketing programmes are based on the fear that the market might see what's really going on inside the company.

29   Elvis said it best: 'We can't go on together with suspicious minds.'

30   Brand loyalty is the corporate version of going steady, but the breakup is inevitable – and coming fast. Because they are networked, smart markets are able to renegotiate relationships with blinding speed.

31   Networked markets can change suppliers overnight. Networked knowledge workers can change employers over lunch. Your own 'downsizing initiatives' taught us to ask the question: 'Loyalty? What's that?'

32   Smart markets will find suppliers who speak their own language.

33   Learning to speak with a human voice is not a parlour trick. It can't be 'picked up' at some tony conference.

34   To speak with a human voice, companies must share the concerns of their communities.

35   But first, they must belong to a community.

36   Companies must ask themselves where their corporate cultures end.

37   If their cultures end before the community begins, they will have no market.

38   Human communities are based on discourse – on human speech about human concerns.

39   The community of discourse *is* the market.

40   Companies that do not belong to a community of discourse will die.

41   Companies make a religion of security, but this is largely a red herring. Most are protecting less against competitors than against their own market and workforce.

42   As with networked markets, people are also talking to each other directly *inside* the company – and not just about rules and regulations, boardroom directives, bottom lines.

43   Such conversations are taking place today on corporate intranets. But only when the conditions are right.

44   Companies typically install intranets top-down to distribute HR policies and other corporate information that workers are doing their best to ignore.

45   Intranets naturally tend to route around boredom. The best are built bottom-up by engaged individuals cooperating to construct something far more valuable: an intranetworked corporate conversation.

46   A healthy intranet *organises* workers in many meanings of the word. Its effect is more radical than the agenda of any union.

47   While this scares companies witless, they also depend heavily on open intranets to generate and share critical knowledge. They need to resist the urge to 'improve' or control these networked conversations.

48   When corporate intranets are not constrained by fear and legalistic rules, the type of conversation they encourage sounds remarkably like the conversation of the networked marketplace.

49   Organisation charts worked in an older economy where plans could be fully understood from atop steep management pyramids and detailed work orders could be handed down from on high.

50   Today, the organisation chart is hyperlinked, not hierarchical. Respect for hands-on knowledge wins over respect for abstract authority.

51   Command-and-control management styles both derive from and reinforce bureaucracy, power tripping and an overall culture of paranoia.

52   Paranoia kills conversation. That's its point. But lack of open conversation kills companies.

53   There are two conversations going on. One inside the company. One with the market.

54   In most cases, neither conversation is going very well. Almost invariably, the cause of failure can be traced to obsolete notions of command and control.

55   As policy, these notions are poisonous. As tools, they are broken. Command and control are met with hostility by intranetworked knowledge workers and generate distrust in internetworked markets.

56   These two conversations want to talk to *each other*. They are speaking the same language. They recognise each other's voices.

57   Smart companies will get out of the way and help the inevitable to happen sooner.

58   If willingness to get out of the way is taken as a measure of IQ, then very few companies have yet wised up.

59   However subliminally at the moment, millions of people now online perceive companies as little more than quaint legal fictions that are actively preventing these conversations from intersecting.

60   This is suicidal. Markets *want* to talk to companies.

61   Sadly, the part of the company a networked market wants to talk to is usually hidden behind a smokescreen of hucksterism, of language that rings false – and often is.

62   Markets do not want to talk to flacks and hucksters. They want to participate in the conversations going on behind the corporate firewall.

63   De-cloaking, getting personal: We *are* those markets. We want to talk to *you*.

64   We want access to your corporate information, to your plans and strategies, your best thinking, your genuine knowledge. We will not settle for the four-colour brochure, for Web sites chock-a-block with eye candy but lacking any substance.

65   We're also the workers who make your companies go. We want to talk to customers directly in our own voices, not in platitudes written into a script.

66   As markets, as workers, both of us are sick to death of getting our information by remote control. Why do we need faceless annual reports and third-hand market research studies to introduce us to each other?

67   As markets, as workers, we wonder why you're not listening. You seem to be speaking a different language.

68   The inflated self-important jargon you sling around – in the press, at your conferences – what's that got to do with us?

69   Maybe you're impressing your investors. Maybe you're impressing Wall Street. You're not impressing us.

70   If you don't impress us, your investors are going to take a bath. Don't they understand this? If they did, they wouldn't *let* you talk that way.

71   Your tired notions of 'the market' make our eyes glaze over. We don't recognise ourselves in your projections – perhaps because we know we're already elsewhere.

72   We like this new marketplace much better. In fact, we are creating it.

73   You're invited, but it's our world. Take your shoes off at the door. If you want to barter with us, get down off that camel!

74   We are immune to advertising. Just forget it.

75   If you want us to talk to you, tell us something. Make it something interesting for a change.

76   We've got some ideas for you too: some new tools we need, some better service. Stuff we'd be willing to pay for. Got a minute?

77   You're too busy 'doing business' to answer our e-mail? Oh gosh, sorry, gee, we'll come back later. Maybe.

78   You want us to pay? We want you to pay attention.

79   We want you to drop your trip, come out of your neurotic self-involvement, join the party.

80   Don't worry, you can still make money. That is, as long as it's not the only thing on your mind.

81   Have you noticed that, in itself, money is kind of one-dimensional and boring? What else can we talk about?

82   Your product broke. Why? We'd like to ask the guy who made it. Your corporate strategy makes no sense. We'd like to have a chat with your CEO. What do you mean she's not in?

83   We want you to take 50 million of us as seriously as you take one reporter from The Wall Street Journal.

84   We know some people from your company. They're pretty cool online. Do you have any more like that you're hiding? Can they come out and play?

85   When we have questions we turn to each other for answers. If you didn't have such a tight rein on 'your people' maybe they'd be among the people we'd turn to.

86   When we're not busy being your 'target market', many of us *are* your people. We'd rather be talking to friends online than watching the clock. That would get your name around better than your entire million-dollar Web site. But you tell us speaking to the market is Marketing's job.

87   We'd like it if you got what's going on here. That'd be real nice. But it would be a big mistake to think we're holding our breath.

88   We have better things to do than worry about whether you'll change in time to get our business. Business is only a part of our lives. It seems to be all of yours. Think about it: who needs whom?

89   We have real power and we know it. If you don't quite see the light, some other outfit will come along that's more attentive, more interesting, more fun to play with.

90   Even at its worst, our newfound conversation is more interesting than most trade shows, more entertaining than any TV sitcom, and certainly more true-to-life than the corporate Web sites we've been seeing.

91   Our allegiance is to ourselves – our friends, our new allies and acquaintances, even our sparring partners. Companies that have no part in this world, also have no future.

92   Companies are spending billions of dollars on Y2K. Why can't they hear this market timebomb ticking? The stakes are even higher.

93   We're both inside companies and outside them. The boundaries that separate our conversations look like the Berlin Wall today, but they're really just an annoyance. We know they're coming down. We're going to work from both sides to *take* them down.

94   To traditional corporations, networked conversations may appear confused, may sound confusing. But we are organising faster than they are. We have better tools, more new ideas, no rules to slow us down.

95   We are waking up and linking to each other. We are watching. But we are not waiting.

The elevator rap

WHEN **Internetworked** *meet* **Intranetworked**
markets workers

The connectedness of the Web is transforming what's inside and outside your business – your market and your employees.

Through the Internet, the people in your markets are discovering and inventing new ways to converse. They're talking about your business. They're telling one another the truth, in very human voices.

Intranets are enabling your best people to hyperlink themselves together, outside the organisation chart. They're incredibly productive and innovative. They're telling one another the truth, in very human voices.

There's a new conversation between and among your market and your workers. It's making them smarter and it's enabling them to discover their human voices.

You have two choices. You can continue to lock yourself behind facile corporate words and happytalk brochures…

Or you can join the conversation.

INTRODUCTION

WHAT IF THE REAL ATTRACTION of the Internet is not its cutting-edge bells and whistles, its jazzy interface or any of the advanced technology that underlies its pipes and wires? What if, instead, the attraction is an atavistic throwback to the prehistoric human fascination with telling tales? Five thousand years ago, the marketplace was the hub of civilisation, a place to which traders returned from remote lands with exotic spices, silks, monkeys, parrots, jewels – and fabulous stories.

In many ways, the Internet more resembles an ancient bazaar than it fits the business models companies try to impose upon it. Millions have flocked to the Net in an incredibly short time, not because it was user-friendly – it wasn't – but because it seemed to offer some intangible quality long missing in action from modern life. In sharp contrast to the alienation wrought by homogenised broadcast media, sterilised mass 'culture', and the enforced anonymity of bureaucratic organisations, the Internet connected people to each other and provided a space in which the human voice would be rapidly rediscovered.

Though corporations insist on seeing it as one, the new marketplace is not necessarily a market at all. To its inhabitants, it is primarily a place in which all participants are audience to each other. The entertainment is not packaged; it is intrinsic. Unlike the lockstep conformity imposed by television, advertising and corporate propaganda, the Net has given new legitimacy – and free rein – to play. Many of those drawn into this world find themselves exploring a freedom never before imagined: to indulge their curiosity, to debate, to disagree, to laugh at themselves, to compare visions, to learn, to create new art, new knowledge.

Because the Internet is so technically efficient, it has also been adopted by companies seeking to become more productive. They too are hungry for knowledge, for the intellectual capital that has become more valuable than bricks and mortar or any tangible asset. What they didn't count on were the other effects of Web technology. Hypertext is inherently nonhierarchical and antibureaucratic. It does not reinforce loyalty and obedience; it encourages idle speculation and loose talk. It encourages stories.

These new conversations online – whether on the wild and woolly Internet or on (slightly) more sedate corporate intranets – are generating new ways of looking at problems. They are spawning new perspectives, new tools and a new kind of intellectual bravery more comfortable with risk than with regulation. The result is not just new things learned but a vastly enhanced ability to learn things. And the pace of this learning is accelerating. In the networked marketplace it is reflected in the joy of play. On company intranets it is reflected in the joy of knowledge. But it's getting difficult to tell the two apart. Employees go home and get online. They bring new attitudes back to work the next day. Enthusiastic surfers get hired and bring strange new views into corporations that, until now, have successfully protected themselves from everything else. The World Wide Web reinforces freedom. The Internet routes around obstacles. The confluence of these conversations is not only inevitable, it has largely already occurred.

Many companies fear these changes, seeing in them only a devastating loss of control. But control is a losing game in a global marketplace where the range of customer choice is already staggering and a suicidal game for companies that must come up with the knowledge necessary to create those market choices.

While command and control may have reached a cul-de-sac, the intersection of the market conversation with the conversation of the corporate workforce hardly signals the end of commerce. Instead, this convergence promises a vibrant renewal in which commerce becomes far more naturally integrated into the life of individuals and communities.

This book tells a story. Four times. Many times. It is the story of how these things have happened – and some powerful hints about what could happen from here on in.

CHAPTER

Internet apocalypso

CHRISTOPHER LOCKE

You set my desire ...
I trip through your wires

U2

Premature burial

WE DIE.

You will never hear those words spoken in a television ad. Yet this central fact of human existence colours our world and how we perceive ourselves within it. 'Life is too short', we say, and it is. Too short for office politics, for busywork and pointless paper chases, for jumping through hoops and covering our asses, for trying to please, to not offend, for constantly struggling to achieve some ever-receding definition of success. Too short as well for worrying whether we bought the right suit, the right breakfast cereal, the right laptop computer, the right brand of underarm deodorant.

Life is too short because we die. Alone with ourselves, we sometimes stop to wonder what's important, really. Our kids, our friends, our lovers, our losses?

Things change and change is often painful. People get 'downsized', move away, the old neighbourhood isn't what it used to be. Children get sick, get better, get bored, get on our nerves. They grow up hearing news of a world more frightening than anything in ancient fairy tales. The wicked witch won't really push you into the oven, honey, but watch out for AK-47s at recess.

Amazingly, we learn to live with it. Human beings are incredibly resilient. We know it's all temporary, that we can't freeze the good times or hold back the bad. We roll with the punches, regroup, rebuild, pick up the pieces, take another shot. We come to understand that life is just like that. And this seemingly simple understanding is the seed of a profound wisdom.

It is also the source of a deep hunger that pervades modern life – a longing for something entirely different from the reality reinforced by everyday experience. We long for more connection between what we do for a living and what we genuinely care about, for work that's more than clock-watching drudgery. We long for release from anonymity, to be seen as who we feel ourselves to be rather than as the sum of abstract metrics and parameters. We long to be part of a world that makes sense rather than accept the accidental alienation imposed by market forces too large to grasp, to even contemplate.

And this longing is not mere wistful nostalgia, not just some unreconstructed adolescent dream. It is living evidence of heart, of what makes us most human.

But companies don't like us human. They leverage our longing for their own ends. If we feel inadequate, there's a product that will fill the hole, a bit of fetishistic magic that will make us complete. Perhaps a new car would do the trick. Maybe a trip to the Caribbean or that new CD or a nice shiny set of Ginsu steak knives. Anything, everything, just get more stuff. Our role is to consume.

Of course, the new car alone is not enough. It must be made to represent something larger. Much larger. The blonde draped over the hood looks so much better than the old lady bitching about the dishes. Surely *she'd* understand our secret needs. And if we showed up with her at the big golf game, wouldn't the guys be impressed! Yeah, gotta get one-a those babies. This isn't about sex, it's about *power* – the greatest bait there ever was to seduce the powerless.

Or take it one slice closer to the bone. Leverage care. For the cost of a jar of peanut butter, you can be a 'Great Mom', the kind every kid would love to have. You can look out on your happy kids playing in that perfect suburban backyard and breathe a little sigh of contentment that life's so good, with not a wicked witch in sight. Just like on television.

We die. And there's more than one way to get it over with. Advertising has some serving suggestions for your premature burial.

Testing, testing ...

But what's this got to do with the Internet? A lot.

The Net grew like a weed between the cracks in the monolithic steel-and-glass empire of traditional commerce. It was technically obscure, impenetrable, populated by geeks and wizards, loners, misfits. When I started using the Internet, nobody gave a damn about it outside of a few big universities and the military-industrial complex they served. In fact, if you were outside that favoured circle, you couldn't even log on. The idea that the Internet would someday constitute the world's largest marketplace would have been laughable if anyone was entertaining such delusions back then. I began entertaining them publicly in 1992 and the laughter was long and loud.

The Net grew and prospered largely because it was ignored. It worked by different rules than the rules of business. Market penetration wasn't interesting because there *was* no market – unless it was a market for new ideas. The Net was built by people who said things like: What if we try this? Nope. What if we try that? Nope. What if we try this other thing? Well, hot damn! Look at that!

One of the hottest damns was the World Wide Web. It came out of efforts to create electronic footnotes – references between academic papers on high-energy physics that maybe a few dozen people in the entire world could actually understand. That's why now, when you turn on your TV, you see www.lastminute.com.

Well, OK, a few things did happen in between. One of those things was that the Internet attracted millions. Many millions. The interesting question to ask is why.

In the early 1990s, there was nothing like the Internet we take for granted today. Back then, the Net was primitive, daunting, uninviting. So what did we come for? And the answer is: each other.

The Internet became a place where people could talk to other people without constraint. Without filters or censorship or official sanction – and perhaps most significantly, without advertising. Another, noncommercial culture began forming across this out-of-the-way collection of computer networks. Long before graphical user interfaces made the scene, the scene was populated by plain old boring ASCII: green phosphor text scrolling up screens at the glacial pace afforded by early modems. So where was the attraction in that?

The attraction was in speech, however mediated. In people talking, however slowly. And mostly, the attraction lay in the kinds of things they were saying. Never in history had so many had the chance to know what so many others were thinking on such a wide range of subjects. Slowly at first, a new kind of conversation was beginning to emerge, but it would achieve global reach with astonishing speed.

In the early days, the Internet was used almost exclusively for government-funded projects and the sort of communication that went along with such work. Here's the new program. It needs some work. There's a bug in the frimular module. Yawn.

But you know what they say about all work and no play. People began to play. Left to themselves, they always do. And the people building the Internet were pretty much left to themselves. They were creating the gameboard. No one else knew how the hell this thing worked, so no one could tell them what they could and couldn't do. They did whatever they liked. And one of the things they liked most was arguing.

Consider that these early denizens of the Net were, for the most part, young, brash, untrained in the intricate dance of corporate politics and highly knowledgeable of their craft. In the prized and noble older sense of the term, they were hackers, and proud of it. Many, in their own assessment if not that of others, were net.gods – high priests of an arcane art very few even knew existed. When disagreements arose over serious matters – the correct use of quotation marks, say – they would join in battle like old Norse warriors:

'Jim, you are a complete idiot. Your code is so brain-damaged it won't even compile. Read a book, moron.'

Today, we tend to think of 'flaming' as a handful of people vociferously insulting each other online. A certain sense of finesse has largely been lost. In the olden days, a good flame war could go on for weeks or months, with hot invective flying around like rhetorical shrapnel. It was high art, high entertainment. Though tempers flared hot and professional bridges were sometimes irreparably burned, ultimately it was a game – a participatory sport in which the audience awarded points for felicitous disparagements, particularly well-worded putdowns, inspired squelches.

It was not a game, however, for the meek of heart. These engagements could be fierce. Even trying to separate the contestants could bring down a hail of sharp-tongued derision. Theories were floated and defended with extreme energy and enthusiasm, if not always with logical rigour. Opinions tended to run high on any given topic. Say you'd posted about your dog. And, look, you got a response! 'Jim, you are a complete idiot. Your dog is so brain-damaged it won't even hunt ...'

If you'd happened to see the first version of the comment to Jim, you might grin at the second. If not, your mileage might vary. But the point is not to extol flame wars, as amusing as some could be. Instead, it is to suggest a particular set of values that began to emerge in what linguists might call a well-bounded speech community. On the Net, you said what you meant and had better be ready to explain your position and how you'd arrived at it. Mouthing platitudes guaranteed that you would be challenged. Nothing was accepted at face value, or taken for granted. Everything was subject to question, revision, re-implementation, parody – whether it was an algorithm, a political philosophy or, God help you, an advertisement.

While the outcome of these debates did not invariably constitute wisdom for the ages, the process by which they took place was honing a razor-sharp sense of collective potential. The conversation was not only engaging, interesting, exciting – it was effective. Tools and techniques emerged with a speed that broke all precedents. As would soon become obvious, the Net was a powerful multiplier for intellectual capital.

Waiting for Joe Six-Pack

A few years ago, you could make an interesting distinction between people who thought there was something special about the Internet and those who saw it as no big deal. Now of course, everybody sees it as a big deal, mostly because of those weirdball IPOs and the overnight billionaires they've spawned. But I think the distinction is still valid. Most companies with Net-dot-dollar-signs in their eyes today are still missing the 'something special' dimension.

Yahoo has already made it, financially speaking, but forms a good example nonetheless. Despite the funky hacker roots of the initial directory Yang and Filo built, Yahoo now describes itself as a 'global media company', thus claiming a closer spiritual kinship with Disney and Murdoch than with the culture that originally put it on the map.

To this mindset, the Net is just an extension of preceding mass media, primarily television. The rhetoric it uses is freighted with the same crypto-religious marketing jargon that characterised broadcast: brand, market share, eyeballs, demographics. And guess what? It works. If nobody was getting rich off this stuff, you wouldn't hear about it.

It's the fast new companies that are reaping these monetary rewards. But guess what again. They're reaping them from an even faster market – one that, for the most part, has only discovered the Internet in the last year or so. The people who make up this new market naturally bring a lot of baggage from their previous experience of mass media. To someone who just got an AOL account last Christmas, I suppose a Web page looks like a v-e-r-y s-l-o-w TV show.

But this is where the something-special effect comes in. It is assumed in some quarters that if you missed the early days of Usenet and didn't use Lynx from a Unix command line, you missed the Magic of Internet Culture. I don't think so.

Sure those were very different days and there was a certain fervour – almost a fever – that was hard to mistake for sitcom fandom. But I think the Internet still has a radicalising effect today, despite all the banner ads and promotional hype and you-may-already-be-a-winner sweepstakes.

The something special is what the Manifesto calls *voice*.

Imagine for a moment: millions of people sitting in their shuttered homes at night, bathed in that ghostly blue television aura. They're passive, yeah, but more than that: they're isolated from each other.

Now imagine another magic wire strung from house to house, hooking all these poor bastards up. They're still watching the same old crap. Then, during the touching love scene, some joker lobs an off-colour aside – and everybody hears it. Whoa! What was that? People are rolling on the floor laughing. And it begins to happen so often, it gets abbreviated: ROTFL. The audience is suddenly connected to *itself*.

What was once The Show, the hypnotic focus and tee-vee advertising carrier wave, becomes in the context of the Internet a sort of reverse new-media McGuffin – an excuse to get together rather than an excuse not to. Think of Joel and the 'bots on *Mystery Science Theater 3000*. The point is not to watch the film, but to outdo each other making fun of it.

And for such radically realigned purposes, some bloated corporate Web site can serve as a target every bit as well as *Godzilla, King of the Monsters*. As the remake trailer put it: size *does* matter.

So here comes Joe Six-Pack onto AOL. What does he know about netliness? Nothing. Zilch. He has no cultural context whatsoever. But soon, very soon, what he hears is something he never heard in TV Land: people cracking up. 'That ain't no laugh track neither,' Joe is thinking and goes looking for the source of this strange, new, rather seductive sound.

So here's a little story problem for you. If the Internet has 50 million people on it, and they're not all as dumb as they look, but the corporations trying to make a fast buck off their asses *are* as dumb as they look, how long before Joe is laughing as hard as everyone else?

The correct answer of course: not long at all. And as soon as he starts laughing, he's not Joe Six-Pack any more. He's no longer part of some passive couch-potato target demographic. Because the Net connects people to *each other*, and impassions and empowers through those connections, the media dream of the Web as another acquiescent mass-consumer market is a figment and a fantasy.

The Internet is inherently seditious. It undermines unthinking respect for centralised authority, whether that 'authority' is the neatly homogenised voice of broadcast advertising or the smarmy rhetoric of the corporate annual report.

And Internet technology has also threaded its way deep into the heart of Corporate Empire, where once upon a time, lockstep loyalty to the chairman's latest attempt at insight was no further away than the mimeograph machine. One memo from Mr Big and everyone believed (or so Mr Big liked to think).

No more. The same kind of seditious deconstruction that's being practised on the Web today, just for the hell of it, is also seeping onto the company intranet. How many satires are floating around there, one wonders: of the latest hyperinflated restructuring plan, of the over-sincere cultural-sensitivity training sessions Human Resources made mandatory last week, of all the gibberish that passes for 'management' – or *has* passed up until now.

Step back a frame or two. Zoom out. Isn't that weird? Workers and markets are speaking the same language! And they're both speaking it in the same shoot-from-the-hip, unedited, devil-take-the-hindmost style.

This conversation may be irreverent of eternal verities, but it's not all jokes. Whether in the marketplace or at work, people do have genuine, serious concerns. And we have something else as well: knowledge. Not the sort of boring, abstract knowledge that 'Knowledge Management' wants to manage. No. The real thing. We have knowledge of what we do and how we do it – our craft – and it drives our voices; it's what we most like to talk about.

But this whole gamut of conversation, from infinite jest to point-specific expertise: who needs it?

Companies need it. Without it they can't innovate, build consensus, or go to market. Markets need it. Without it they don't know what works and what doesn't; don't know why they should give a damn. Cultures need it. Without play and knowledge in equal measure, they begin to die. People get gloomy, anxious and depressed. Eventually, the guns come out.

There are two new conversations going on today, both vibrant and exciting; both mediated by Internet technologies but having little to do with technology otherwise. Unfortunately, there's also a metaphorical firewall separating these conversations, and that wall is the traditional, conservative, fearful corporation.

So what is to be done? Easy: Burn down business-as-usual. Bulldoze it. Cordon off the area. Set up barricades. Cripple the tanks. Topple the statues of heroes too long dead into the street.

Sound familiar? You bet it does. And the message has been the same all along, from Paris in '68 to the Berlin Wall, from Warsaw to Tiananmen Square: Let the kids rock and roll!

So open the windows and turn up the volume. If the noise gets loud enough, maybe even CNN will cover it.

From ancient markets to global networks

This may seem rabidly antibusiness. It's not. Business is just a word for buying and selling things. In one way or another, we all rely on this commerce, both to get the things we want or need, and to afford them. We are alternately the workers who create products and services, and the customers who purchase them. There is nothing inherently wrong with this setup. Except when it becomes all of life. Except when life becomes secondary and subordinate. At the beginning of the 21st century, business so dominates all other aspects of our existence that it's hard to imagine it was ever otherwise. But it was. Imagine it.

Storylines

A few thousand years ago there was a marketplace. Never mind where. Traders returned from far seas with spices, silks and precious, magical stones. Caravans arrived across burning deserts bringing dates and figs, snakes, parrots, monkeys, strange music, stranger tales. The marketplace was the heart of the city, the kernel, the hub, the *omphalos*. Like past and future, it stood at the crossroads. People woke early and went there for coffee and vegetables, eggs and wine, for pots and carpets, rings and necklaces, for toys and sweets, for love, for rope, for soap, for wagons and carts, for bleating goats and evil-tempered camels. They went there to look and listen and to marvel, to buy and be amused. But mostly they went to meet each other. And to talk.

In the market, language grew. Became bolder, more sophisticated. Leaped and sparked from mind to mind. Incited by curiosity and rapt attention, it took astounding risks that none had ever dared to contemplate, built whole civilisations from the ground up.

Markets are conversations. Trade routes pave the storylines. Across the millennia in between, the human voice is the music we have always listened for, and still best understand.

So what went wrong? From the perspective of corporations, many of which by the 20th century had become bigger and far more powerful than ancient city-states, nothing went wrong. But things did change.

Commerce is a natural part of human life, but it has become increasingly unnatural over the intervening centuries, incrementally divorcing itself from the people on whom it most depends, whether workers or customers. While this change is in many ways understandable – huge factories took the place of village shops; the marketplace moved from the centre of the town and came to depend on far-flung mercantile trade – the result has been to interpose a vast chasm between buyers and sellers.

By our own lifetimes, mass production and mass media had totally transformed this relationship, which came to be characterised by alienation and mystery. Exactly what relationship did producers and markets have to each other any more? In attempting to answer this blind-man's-bluff question, market research became a billion-dollar industry.

Once an intrinsic part of the local community, commerce has evolved to become the primary force shaping the community of nations on a global scale. But because of its increasing divorce from the day-to-day concerns of real people, commerce has come to ignore the natural conversation that defines communities as human.

The slow pace of this historic change has made it seem unsurprising to many that people are now valued primarily for their capacity to consume, as targets for product pitches, as demographic abstractions. Few living in the so-called civilised world today can envision commerce as ever having been anything different. But much of the change happened in the century just passed.

Economies of scale: mo' bigga mo' betta

The Internet is often seen as a unique phenomenon that only recently burst into the economic mainstream. But looking at the Net in strictly technological terms obscures its relationship to broader economic trends that were already well under way.

By the end of the 19th century, the United States was poised to become the prototypical mass market. It had vast natural resources, a fast-growing population and a contiguous geography generally unbounded by tariff restrictions. Cheap iron coupled with a voracious appetite for industrial expansion enabled a railway system capable of cost-effectively delivering goods to nearly every part of a captive domestic market.

Given the high cost of entry into such enterprises, and without appreciable foreign competition, manufacturers cared little about product differentiation. Thus Henry Ford's attitude towards customer choice: 'They can have any colour they want as long as it's black.' More than for his wit, Ford is remembered for designing the first high-volume automotive assembly lines. The more cars Ford could make, the lower the unit cost and the greater the margin of profit. These economies of scale led to enormous profits because they enabled selling a far cheaper product to a far wider market.

Ford was strongly influenced by Frederick Taylor and his theory of 'scientific management'. Taylor's time-and-motion metrics sought to bring regularity and predictability to bear on the increasingly detailed division of labour. Under such a regimen, previously holistic craft expertise rapidly degraded into the mindless execution of single repetitive tasks, with each worker performing only one operation in the overall process. Because of its effect on workers' knowledge, *de-skilling* is a term strongly associated with mass production. And as skill disappeared, so did the unique voice of the craftsman.

The organisation was elegantly simple, if not terribly humane. Atop the management hierarchy resided near-omniscient knowledge of products and manufacturing methods. In the case of Ford, product design, process design, marketing strategy and other critical functions were chiefly the province of one man, Henry. This knowledge was translated into work orders that were executed by an increasingly layered cadre of lieutenants who directed a large but largely unskilled workforce. This style of command-and-control management worked best for single product-lines with few parts and simple processes.

Economies of scope: would you like fries with that?

Mass production, mass marketing and mass media have constituted the Holy Trinity of American business for at least a hundred years. The payoffs were so huge that the mindset became an addiction, a drug blinding its users to changes that began to erode the old axioms attaching to economies of scale.

These changes were gradual at first. Even early on, 'economies of scope' began to be perceived. General Motors broke Ford's run on the Model-T – an impossibly long product cycle by today's standards – by offering cars that were not black, and even came in different styles to suit different tastes and pocketbooks. Heinz discovered it could make not just, say, mustard, but '57 Varieties' of condiments in the same factory. Consumers began to have a wider range of choice, and they warmed quickly to their new options.

But things got more complicated on the management side. As more products were launched, organisations became increasingly bureaucratic and business functions more isolated from each other. This was de-skilling of a higher order: design, production and marketing knowledge began to fractionate and, in some cases, to atrophy.

The real watershed came when offshore producers, finally recovered from the Second World War, began to penetrate US markets. With the oil embargo of the early 1970s, small, fuel-efficient cars began looking highly attractive to people stalled in long gas lines. Companies like Honda, Toyota and Volkswagen exploded into the North American market like a tsunami. The challenge to US manufacturers was not to offer just trivial feature alternatives, but whole new designs. In a classic reversal, what was suddenly good for America was anything but good for General Motors. The auto industry didn't see these changes coming and, as a result, lost enormous market share to offshore competitors.

Overnight, global competition turned mass markets into thousands of micro markets. Nike now makes hundreds of different styles of shoes. The Wall Street Journal coined the term *sneakerization* to describe a phenomenon affecting nearly every industry.

Competition is healthy, we'd been told from birth, because it breeds greater choice. But now competition was out of control and old-guard notions of brand allegiance evaporated like mist in the rising-sun onslaught from Japan, South-east Asia and Europe. Choice and quality ruled the day, and consumer enthusiasm for the resulting array of new product options forever undermined the foundations of yesterday's mass-market economy.

The relentless search for market niches drove a steep increase in new product introductions, which in turn required an exponential increase in design and process knowledge. There were just two problems. First, mass-production-oriented business processes had been 'stove-piped' into noncommunicating bureaucratic business functions. Second, workers long told to 'check your brain at the door', were ill-equipped for the dynamic changes about to wreak havoc on the corporation.

In short, command-and-control management didn't work so well any more. Necessary knowledge no longer resided at the top. It was as if the organisational core had melted down, and companies that couldn't adjust fast enough – or that were culturally unwilling to shift gears – went belly up as a result.

Who knows?

This sudden need for more, better, and better distributed knowledge spawned various attempts at a solution. Three are especially noteworthy.

1. **Concurrent engineering:** What if separate functions – say design and manufacturing – talked to each other from the outset of a product cycle? This astoundingly obvious idea hadn't yet occurred to anyone because market hegemony and mass production had made it appear unnecessary. If you made only one product, and it had a long life cycle, there was no problem. However, as products proliferated and life cycles accelerated, the need to manage widely distributed knowledge became intense. While concurrent engineering was a step in the right direction, it assumed there was sufficient knowledge in top-down control functions to specify detailed commands to thousands of workers producing hundreds of different products. Big mistake.

2. **Artificial Intelligence:** Announced with messianic fanfare in the 1980s, this new branch of computer science sought to automate expertise. If 'scientific management' had ramped productivity through the division of physical labour, why not apply the same techniques to intellectual labour? However, if industrial automation is de-skilling, AI is akin to a frontal lobotomy. Instead of distributing knowledge, so-called expert systems made it dependent on complex and inflexible software. In most cases, these programs simply didn't work. Knowledge worthy of the name is highly dynamic. It requires deep understanding, not just rules and algorithms. While machines are lousy at this sort of thing, people are remarkably adaptive and intelligent. People learn. Real expertise is changing too fast today to lend itself to automation.

3. **Total Quality Management:** TQM suggested the unthinkable to companies intent on automating knowledge: why not look to your employees? The basic idea was to empower the people who actually did the work. Knowledge resides within practice – a truth that AI forgot, to its fatal detriment. In companies that adopted some form of TQM, business practices began to resemble older notions of craft instead of the brain-numbing repetition of preordained procedures. People were encouraged to share what they knew with each other, with other departments and divisions, and with the company as a whole. This exchange became a rapidly expanding conversation – a conversation that would soon populate the corporate intranet.

Understanding, learning, exploration, curiosity, collaboration – qualities that had been bred out of workers by industrial management – were now being desperately elicited by the All-New, Culturally Revolutionised Organisation. Many spouted the new religion, but secretly tried to hedge old bureaucratic bets. A handful walked the talk, but it was tough going. A central tenet of TQM was W. Edwards Deming's dictum: 'Drive Out Fear' – a challenge that went to the heart of the corporation. Conversations among workers were finally seen as critical to the spread of valuable knowledge – 'best practices' in the still-current jargon. Conversations are where intellectual capital gets generated. But business environments based on command-and-control are usually characterised by intimidation, coercion and threats of reprisal. In contrast, genuine conversation flourishes only in an atmosphere of free and open exchange.

Enter the Internet

Our whirlwind historical tour has focused on manufacturing because that sector was first to experience these changes. Later, the same forces began to reshape service and information industries. The Internet not only arrived into the context of a newly globalised economy, it has been profoundly shaped by it. Companies installing intranets are seeking to capture and preserve critical knowledge. Individuals coming onto the Internet are seeking the same range of choice that was first offered by imported cars and stereo equipment.

However, most 'e-commerce' plays today look a lot like General Motors circa 1969 – looking for that next lucrative mass market just when markets have shattered into a million mirror-shard constituencies, many asking for something altogether different from the mindless razzle-dazzle of the tube. Marketeers still drool at the prospect of the Net replicating the top-down broadcast model wherein glitzy 'content' is developed at great cost in remote studios and jammed down a one-way pipe into millions of living rooms. TV with a buy button! Wowee!

Today, many large companies offer flashy bread-and-circus entertainments on the Web. These offerings have all the classic earmarks of the mass market come-on: lowest-common-denominator programming developed to package and deliver market segments to mass merchandisers. This is not what most people want, or they would have stuck with television, the Yellow Pages and 0800 numbers. And they don't have to accept it since the Internet came up with the concept of infinite channel-surfing.

The Net represents cheap natural resources (data), cheap transport (the pipe itself), and most important, cheap and efficient access to global know-how. The barriers to entry have fallen so low that a huge number of companies can now compete for a niche – an influx that echoes the entry of Asian and European competitors into US markets. But this is more like an invasion from outer space: 10 000 saucers just landed and they're merely the advance wave.

Just as GM mistook the Hondas and VWs for a passing fad, most corporations today are totally misreading this invasion from Webspace. Their brand will save them. Right. Their advertising budget will save them. Uh-huh. More bandwidth will save them. Sure. Well ... something will save them. They're just not too sure what it is yet. But the clock is now ticking in Internet time. Maybe they should get a clue. And quick.

Border crossings

To most large traditional companies, the notion that workers might actually know what they were doing was a huge insight. (Duh!) But it takes hard work to implement the changes required to elicit knowledge from employees. In most cases, that work is not only incomplete, it hasn't even begun. 'Drive out fear?' Dream on.

Knowledge worth having comes from turned-on volitional attention, not from slavishly following someone else's orders. Innovation based on such knowledge is exciting, inflammatory, even 'dangerous', because it tends to challenge fixed procedures and inflexible policies. While collaboration has been paid much lip service within corporations, few have attempted it beyond their own boundaries. Ironically, companies that remain 'secure' within those boundaries will be cut off from the global marketplace with which they must engage in order to survive and prosper.

And this engagement must be fearless and far-reaching. Workers must become fully empowered and self-directed. Scary. Suppliers must become trusted allies in developing new products and business strategies. Scarier still. Markets must come to have faces and personalities in place of statistical profiles. Flat-out panic!

For many, the new landscape is barely recognisable, online or off. Where business is headed there are no roadmaps yet, and few comforting parallels with the past. The landscape has little to do with mass production, mass merchandising, mass markets, mass media or mass culture.

Instead, the future business of businesses that have a future will be about subtle differences, not wholesale conformity; about diversity, not homogeneity; about breaking rules, not enforcing them; about pushing the envelope, not punching the clock; about invitation, not protection; about doing it first, not doing it 'right'; about making it better, not making it perfect; about telling the truth, not spinning bigger lies; about turning people on, not 'packaging' them; and perhaps above all, about building convivial communities and knowledge ecologies, not leveraging demographic sectors.

The new workplace: breaking the silence

Let us speak, though we show all our faults
and weaknesses – for it is a sign of strength
to be weak, to know it, and out with it ...

Herman Melville

Just as traditional media conditioned the audience to be passive consumers – first of commercial messages, then of products – the traditional organisation conditioned employees to be obedient executors of bureaucratically disseminated work orders. Both are forms of broadcast: the few dictating the behaviour of the many. The broadcast mentality isn't dead by any means. It's just become suicidal.

In contrast, the Internet invites participation. It is genuinely empowering, well beyond the cliché that word has become. And corporate intranets invite participation in the same way. There are strong reciprocal parallels between the open-ended curiosity of the new marketplace and the knowledge requirements of the new organisation. The market-oriented Internet and workforce-focused intranet each relies on the other in fundamental and highly complementary ways. Without strong market objectives and connections, there is no viable focus for a company's

Internet presence; without a strong intranet, market objectives and connections remain wishful thinking.

The same technology that has opened up a new kind of conversation in the marketplace has done the same within the corporation, or has the potential to do so. But many businesses, especially large ones, still refuse to acknowledge these radical shifts affecting internal workforces and external markets. They don't want to relinquish hierarchic control. They don't want to give up the tremendous economies of scale they enjoyed under the old-school broadcast-advertising alliance. It's what they know. It's how they made their fortunes. However, trying to keep things in the old familiar business-as-usual rut denies the ability of markets to respond to and interact with companies directly – and this is what the Internet has brought to the party.

Why the denial? Could it be that companies are afraid the Internet and intranets will make people smarter? While no company would ever admit to it publicly, this is precisely what many fear. In the 'good old days', consumers weren't expected to make suggestions or ask for new features. They were simply supposed to buy the product – any colour they wanted as long as it was black. In the same way, workers weren't expected to offer insights or suggestions, just to do what they were told.

Networks greatly facilitate the sharing of relevant knowledge within a community joined by like interests. As a result, the lowest common denominator of informed awareness tends to be much higher online than it ever was in the context of broadcast media. Plus, this informed awareness tends to increase much faster. This accelerated learning effect obviously applies to intranets as well – it's where their primary value lies. But a lot can get in the way of this value before it has a chance to evolve and mature.

In 1995, *Business Week* ran an excellent cover story on intranets, just around the time the buzzword was emerging into general parlance. Several CIOs were quoted as saying they had so-and-so many thousand Web pages behind their firewalls. They were crowing about it. But my take was that this content didn't get created top-down by the organisation. Instead, these pages sprang up overnight like a crop of magic mushrooms on a rich mother lode of corporate horseshit.

What does that mean, you ask? Well, look, when all this got started you had thousands of workers with easy access to free Web browsers and a smaller set of people who had figured out how to set up Web servers whose only cost was download and tinkering time. These people soon figured out that HTML wasn't rocket science, and it was off to the races from there. Suddenly there was nothing to prevent the expression of their own ideas and creativity. Skunkworks wanted to build broader support for their projects, individuals wanted to be noticed for their technical savvy or penetrating wit or business insight.

But then the big-O Organisation discovered what was going on and, often as not, brought all this self-motivated fever-pitch development to a grinding halt. Hey, way to go!

To be fair, there were a few high-level execs out there who truly understood the dynamics of how this stuff worked. And by dynamics, I mean more the cultural aspect of networking. For the technology, you could buy a book. Aside from this handful, though, most corporate managers were clueless in the extreme.

And, sadly, most still are. Too many have never spent any serious time online. Then, when they get charged with building a corporate intranet, the first thing they think about is reporting structures and where everybody will sit in some abstract organisation chart. But dictatorial directives – 'All Web pages must be formally approved by the Department of Business Prevention' – throw cold water onto all that magic-mushroom enthusiasm.

The fact is, people at the bottommost tiers of the organisation often have far more valuable knowledge than managers and corporate control freaks. If you kill off this enthusiasm, you can easily end up with a large, professional-looking and very expensive intranet that nobody gives a damn about. The question companies should be asking themselves is: What if we built an intranet and nobody came?

Top management support needs to come in the form of funding, facilitation and enough brains to get out of the way. It's gotta be more like rock and roll than strait-laced traditional business – and that puts the Suits right over the edge. It's just not possible, they argue, to run a business by letting everybody improvise.

But companies function that way whether anybody wants them to or not. Nobody really runs them; no one writes the score. Corporate management is still largely unaware of what's going on in the marketplace. But their workers know, because they're operating there already. What's going on is the Internet.

Today, market expectations are solidly welded to Net-speed performance. Your software product isn't available for downloading? You don't have secure transaction processing so I can buy it when I need it? Hey, I'm gone! And so is a big chunk of your market share. If your company feeds me a ration of facile hype instead of answering my questions, I'm looking for another supplier.

And the expectation of getting quick, straight answers applies across the board to information of every stripe. It applies to ideas – how to acquire them within the company and from the market, move them around, sort them, slice them, dice them, move them back out into the market as new products, get customer feedback – then iterate, getting better as you go. Make mistakes. Debug on the fly. It's fast, it's furious. It's fun! If you want a rock-and-roll company, which is more important, adhering to procedure or knowing how to dance?

The fervour that produced the first wild-oats crop of intranets surely didn't come from the Chief Information Officers (CIOs) who got quoted in *Business Week*. Workers have had it with repressive management that just gets in the way. Markets have had it with hyperbole-laden corporate rhetoric that's 99 per cent hot air. The next huge opportunity for business is to bring workforce and market together. And companies smart enough to realise this start instigating a potent form of internal anarchy.

Unfortunately, such companies are rare exceptions. Most are hanging on for dear life to the one thing they think they can't live without: control. But they only think they're in control. Feeling their real abilities and contributions have gone unappreciated, many employees simply do what they feel like doing anyway, giving as little as possible to the company. They punch the clock and that's it. The relationship is adversarial as hell. If you look into it closely, though, the company has almost invariably set things up this way – by not trusting people to take the initiative, to be engaged, motivated, intelligent, creative, innovative. It's a long, sad story with roots that go back to the early industrial era.

Corporate intranets represent a prime opportunity to turn this scenario around, but only if there's genuine awareness of where the real challenges lie. Too much of intranet development is focused on whiz-bang technology and not nearly enough on the cultural revolution all this implies and in fact demands.

In healthy intranet environments, work gets co-ordinated via cooperation and negotiation among colleagues. But these things happen very fast, not in committee meetings. This is why employees need more power in organisations – not to lord it over others, but to make intelligent decisions on the fly and not see them overturned two days later by managers who don't know the territory. Without getting into the politics of it, the biggest complaint of the US armed forces in Vietnam was that the war was being fought from Washington. Again without getting into the politics of it: the US lost. This is a big clue as to how many intranet initiatives are playing out. Top-down command-and-control management has become dysfunctional and counterproductive.

Imposed infrastructures hinder more than help. Most so-called empowerment initiatives are embarrassingly paternalistic, to the point of backfiring entirely. Real authority is based on respect for knowledge and the two are inherently intertwined. Also, both grow bottom-up. When arbitrary 'management' takes over what was initially a handcrafted intranet, the individuals who championed and created it often feel betrayed and disenfranchised. You see the same thing in what happened to craft and the individual voice during the course of the Industrial Revolution. We're making some very old mistakes here.

Take another example much closer to the present. The autonomous PC challenged the hegemony of mainframe computer systems and enabled the development of quick solutions that could end-run the infamous MIS-bottleneck – the fact that it could take months for computer applications to be created and executed to deliver needed information. Then IT management discovered the LAN, which delivered another layer of utility. However, instead of leveraging this new resource for the benefit of 'users' – even that word is an artefact of the mentality – the IT department largely used the LAN to re-establish control over information access and work environments.

Now, many companies are doing the same thing again with the intranet. You get this rule-book mindset – the corporation's common look and feel, logo placement, legal number of words on each Web page. Whatever. It's all so cramped and constipated and uninviting. Dead. The people who actually built the intranet – created the content that makes it valuable – bail out, looking for another, more open system. And today that's easy to find.

Remember the context for all this. Twenty years ago, or even five, only corporations could provide the kind of resources needed to process even modest volumes of information. The cost of such systems was a significant barrier to entry for new businesses that might become competitors. But today individuals have this kind of power in their rec rooms. And they can get all the Internet they can eat for a few bucks a month. If the company doesn't come through with the kind of information and delivery that turns them on – provides learning, advances careers and nurtures the unbridled joy of creation – well, hey, they'll just do it elsewhere. Maybe in the garage.

This sort of thing has already been happening for a while now, of course, but there's more on the way, and not just from the usually suspected quarters. To understand what's really happening on the Internet, you have to get down beneath the commercial hype and hoopla, which – though it gets 90 per cent of the press – is actually a late arrival. From the beginning, something very different has been brewing online. It has to do with living, with livelihood, with craft, connection and community. This isn't some form of smarmy New Age mysticism, either. It's tough and gritty and it's just beginning to find its voice, its own direction. But it's also difficult to describe; as the song says, 'It's like trying to tell a stranger about rock and roll'. And it's next to impossible to understand unless you've experienced it for yourself. You have to live in the Net for a while.

At this level, things are often radically other than they appear. A new kind of logic is emerging, or needs to. I call it gonzo business management – paradox becomes paradigm. We're not in Kansas any more, Toto, and we might as well get used to it. There's a huge opportunity here for individuals to keep their day jobs but at the same time to indulge their natural human bent for self-expression.

Companies that try to prevent this sort of creativity within their firewalls need to have their collective heads examined. Conversely, companies that foster and encourage it will win big. The best software, design, music, graphics, writing – elegant, artistic, fantastically interesting and valuable content – are coming out of places where people feel their creativity is valued. Places where inspiration is paramount and posturing means nothing.

Great intranets come from corporate basements, not from boardrooms. How do you know where the next big thing is going to come from? You need great radar today, and that means a wide-awake workforce that's constantly tinkering, exploring and figuring out new ways to have fun.

The long history of distrust between workers and management didn't start with Karl Marx or the unions. It's based more on fallout from the ideas of people like Frederick Taylor and Henry Ford, ideas like 'scientific management' and Theory X. Underlying these questionable principles that have done so much to shape the assumptions of business-as-usual is the premise that workers are lazy, unwilling, even stupid. Today, this premise translates into the near-certainty that employees are pilfering company time, collecting a paycheque while hanging out on the Web all day. They probably are. But that's a symptom, not a cause.

The people who built the first intranets put in ridiculously long days. They worked like soldiers rebuilding a bridge. You had to be there to believe it. But many now managing Internet or intranet projects were not there and they don't believe it. It all goes back to fear of losing control. Whatever the motive, the mentality has to go. Right now these fear-driven corporations are spending millions on market research, the whole point of which is to find out who their customers are. They don't know any more. They've barricaded themselves in their executive suites, and now they've erected firewalls on top of that.

Sure, data security is necessary and needs to be done well. However, many corporations are desperate for firewalls because they don't want the market to see they have nothing worth stealing inside them. That's not security, it's paranoia. You can't identify best practices without sticking your neck out – but if you don't, you risk premature death. You can't invite customers to contribute design ideas by holding them at bay.

And unless your industry is very 'mature' – which really means ready for the bone yard – your market isn't wearing pinstripe suits any more, either. Many companies are currently doing market planning today using straw-man models of the customer that constitute a bad pastiche of Eisenhower-era sitcom outtakes and those throwback Human Resources manuals that haven't been edited in 30 years. Was anybody ever this straight or this stupid? Are they now? If not, what does this say about current approaches to online marketing? In many cases, your workers are your market. Come out of the bunker once in a while, see what they're up to – it could be your future.

But for that to happen, you've to get beyond the firewall. The Internet/intranet dichotomy reinforces the 'not invented here', syndrome that has damaged so many companies. Corporations have long understood that they have to tear down the internal walls that prevent necessary cross-functional communication. Now they have to tear down their external walls as well. The survivors will be left standing naked – the stuff of nightmares for many companies. But they'll be left standing naked in the middle of a thriving marketplace. For businesses capable of grasping the ramifications, this is an enormously promising paradox.

In a networked market, the best way for a company to 'advertise' will be to provide a public window on its intranet. Instead of putting up slick images of what they'd like people to believe, corporations will open up so people can see what's really going on.

Sometime soon, companies will have to open up significant portions of their intranets – while still protecting their few genuine secrets – in order to create relationships with their markets rather than barriers against them. Otherwise, they're saying in effect: 'We know everything we need to know. Why should we look beyond our own borders?' That's just plain wrong, and everybody knows it – especially your workers and your customers.

Companies that are actually communicating with online markets have flung the doors wide open. They're constantly searching for solid information they can share with customers and prospects via Web and FTP sites, e-mail lists, phone calls, whatever it takes. They're not half as concerned with protecting their data as with how much information they can give away. That's how they stay in touch, stay competitive, keep market attention from drifting to competitors. Such companies are creating a new kind of corporate identity, based not on the repetitive advertising needed to create 'brand awareness', but on substantive, personalised communications.

The question is whether, as a company, you can afford to have more than an advertising-jingle persona. Can you put yourself out there: say what you think in your own voice, present who you really are, show what you really care about? Do you have any genuine passion to share? Can you deal with such honesty? Such exposure? Human beings are often magnificent in this regard, while companies, frankly, tend to suck. For most large corporations, even considering these questions – and they're being forced to do so by both Internet and intranet – is about as exciting as the offer of an experimental brain transplant.

But the future looks dismal only to companies that are spooked by the prospect of coming in out of the cold. Those at highest risk aren't wonderful places to be working in at any level today. Their future could be very bright if they'd just decide to stop being prisons with nasty wardens. If they choose not to stop, I don't have much pity. Companies that are harming themselves out of ignorance can, with a little humility and a lot of hard work, begin to learn and change. I've seen it happen, and it's an impressive thing. On the other hand, companies that are harming the people who work for them out of cowardice, greed and wilful stupidity richly deserve whatever fate may have in store.

Giant companies tend to look only over the tops of the trees at other giants they consider worthy competitors. Few bother to look down at their feet. If they did, many would see their foundations being nibbled away by competitors many times smaller, yet fiercely committed to do battle for even a tiny slice of this new territory. Some little garage operation can only take away, say, .001 per cent of market share from one of these monster companies. However, a hundred thousand garage operations can take it all – and given the new business dynamics the Internet brings to bear, this can happen overnight. The Net will cause radical discontinuities, catastrophic breaks in the already crumbling facade of business-as-usual.

Companies currently have a lot of motivation to get serious. And to get really serious, they first have to get a sense of humour and relax – yet another pretzel-logic paradox. They need to relax to break the obsessive-compulsive control habit. They need to understand that employees already know how to do the work far better than the company could ever hope to dictate. Corporate intranets could unleash the potential energy of the corporation, but to nourish and grow that potential, companies have to relinquish their addiction to management. Zen master Suzuki Roshi once said, 'To control your cow, give it a bigger pasture.'

At some point you've got to break down and trust people both inside and outside 'your' organisation – and the Web is responsible for those quotation marks. It is radically blurring the boundaries of what's inside and outside, yours and theirs. The only way companies can sound authentic to new online markets is to empower employees who actually have the knowledge to disseminate it on their behalf. And from here on in, that's always going to mean a two-way street between workplace and marketplace.

The new marketplace: word gets around

In the late 18th century, the British philosopher Jeremy Bentham imagined a little nightmare he called a 'panopticon' – a prison in which the inmates could be seen at all times, but couldn't see their jailers. A few hundred years later, mass media inverted this scenario. The imprisoning TV eye now sees nothing, yet we all watch it for clues to our cultural identity. But what would happen if each of these isolated prison cells was somehow wired to all the rest so the inmates could observe their overseers? Not only see them, but also speculate about their motives, and compare notes on their behaviour and intentions? It's already happened. That's what the Internet does. Suddenly the overseer is like an insect mounted on a pin for all to view.

While corporations are still only marginally aware of what's being said about them online, all but the totally out-of-it are uncomfortably aware these conversations are taking place, and that the control they had in the days of broadcast has evaporated. We're not just watching the ads these days, we're publicly deconstructing them. In this context, intranets look like salvation to many companies, their protective firewalls a form of corporate encryption designed to insulate against a scary new kind of market: unpredictable, unmanageable, unwilling to be manipulated.

At one point the Cluetrain Manifesto says: 'Markets do not want to talk to flacks and hucksters. They want to participate in the conversations going on behind the corporate firewall. De-cloaking, getting personal: We are those markets. We want to talk to you.'

De-cloaking even more: I wrote that last bit. Personally. The Internet has radically changed the nature of the marketplace. I believe this. But how do I presume to know it? Certainly not through market-research reports, most of which aren't worth the paper they're written on. I know it because the Internet has changed me and the thousands of people I talk to every week. Maybe the best way to explain this is to tell my own story – talk about who I am and how I got here. Am I representative of the online market? The point is that there is no 'online market' in some general abstract sense. More than any market that's ever existed, the Internet is a collection of unique individuals. I'm one of them.

I bought my first computer in 1981. It had a 300-baud modem that I used to connect to The Source, the first commercial online service. For those who may not know, *baud* is a technical term meaning 'extremely slow'. Nonetheless, I used this machine to talk to people I'd never met. We'd hook up and say things like: 'Hey, who are you? What's happening over there? And by the way, where is over there?' The personal computer seemed to me the all-purpose machine. You could draw with it, write on it, save thoughts and recall them later, recombine them – you could even make music. I was a carpenter and a cabinetmaker and into tools in a big way. Here was a machine that communicated with others of its type, and behind each one was another person, another mind jamming, improvising, conveying ideas, feelings and experiences I'd never before had a way to tap into. I'd never encountered a tool this powerful.

Through a weird combination of fortuitous accidents, I ended up in Tokyo several years later working in an artificial intelligence project for the Japanese Government. What the project needed – and what I had to offer – was a fairly good grasp of the

English language. What I lacked was any formal training in computer science. Nothing had prepared me for the stratospheric high-tech world I suddenly found myself immersed in. I knew next to nothing about machine intelligence, but I was fascinated by its core concept of 'knowledge engineering'. The challenge was to model how people understand things, represent ideas, and communicate them to others. In this case, the 'other' was a computer. I could relate to the enormity of the problem. I was groping around in the dark myself, struggling with new concepts, and learning as I went. I was flying by the seat of my pants.

One day, I met with a researcher in a coffee shop. Language was a problem, but he spoke more English than I did Japanese. I had just been to the bookstore and was lugging a stack of books on highly advanced computer-science topics. It was all Greek to me, but I figured something might rub off. Suddenly the guy asks me, 'Who gives you permission to read those books?'

I was stunned. Bowled over. Did his puzzlement reflect some sort of cultural difference? I didn't think so. It struck me that this fellow was just being more honest and direct than an American might be. He was articulating what many people in today's world seem to assume: that official authorisation is required to learn new things. I thought about this deeply, and I'm thinking about it still.

Who gives us permission to explore our world? The question implies that the world in fact belongs to someone else. Who gives us permission to communicate what we've experienced, what we believe, what we've discovered of that world for ourselves? The question betokens a history of voice suppressed, of whole cultures that have come to believe only power is sanctioned to speak. Because the ability to speak *does* involve power. It entails ownership and the control conferred by ownership. As the saying has it: 'Money talks, bullshit walks.'

Right then and there, in that chance encounter in some random Tokyo coffee shop, I gave myself blanket permission: to be curious, to learn, to speak, to write. But it's a long road from permission to practice, and there's plenty of negative reinforcement in between. Freedom of expression may be called out loftily in the US Constitution, but even after two centuries of democracy, it's still a far cry from second nature.

Communication is a powerful tool. And like any other powerful tool, it has been pressed into the service of business-as-usual. A few years after my stint in Japan, I ended up back in the United States, hired by an AI software outfit to be their director of corporate communications. Cool, I thought. That sounded important. I had no idea what it meant. Only later did I discover I'd become their PR guy. Bummer.

I was pretty naïve back then, but I quickly figured out that public relations was perceived by the press – the people I was supposed to be talking to – as little more than thinly disguised hucksterism. I tried playing the high-tech huckster role precisely once and came away from the experience feeling dirty, phony. I couldn't bring myself to do it again, which was a big problem. It was my job. And I needed the money. Stop me if any of this sounds familiar.

The 'key messages' of any AI software company back then involved head-bangingly abstruse concepts like 'heuristics', 'backward chaining' and 'nonmonotonic logic'. Very deep. And *very* boring. I barely understood this jargon myself. How was I supposed to get on the phone with some total stranger and enthuse about The Product? The truth was, I didn't give a damn about the product. What I cared about was knowledge, how people acquired and used it, how organisations suddenly seemed to need a lot more of it, and why. What I cared about was how technology applied – or didn't – to the world of business and the actual people who worked there.

So instead of pitching the product, I started talking to journalists about stuff like that. I figured I'd just pretend to be working until I got fired for goofing off. But something amazing happened. As soon as I stopped strategising how to 'get ink' for the company that was paying my salary, as soon as I stopped seeing journalists as a source of free advertising for my employer, I started having genuine conversations with genuinely interesting people.

I'd call up editors and reporters without a thought in my head – no agenda, no objective – and we'd talk. We talked about manufacturing and how it evolved, about shop rats and managers, command and control. We talked about language and literature, about literacy. We talked about software too of course – what it could and couldn't do. We talked about the foibles of the industry itself, laughed about empty buzzwords and pompous posturing, swapped war stories about trade shows and writing on deadline. We talked about our own work. But these conversations weren't work. They were interesting and engaging. They were exciting. They were fun. I couldn't wait to get back to work on Monday morning.

Then something even more amazing happened. The company started 'getting ink'. Lots of it. And not in the lowly trade rags it had been used to, but in places like *The New York Times* and *The Wall Street Journal* and *Business Week*. One day the CEO called the VP of Marketing into my office.

'What has Chris been doing for you lately?' the CEO asked him.

'I'm glad you brought that up,' said the marketing VP. 'In the whole time he's been here, he hasn't done a single thing I've asked him to.'

'Well ...' said the CEO looking down at his shoes – here it comes, I thought, this is what it feels like to get sacked – 'whatever it is he's doing, leave him alone. From now on, he reports to me.'

That's how I discovered PR doesn't work and that markets are conversations.

That's also how I started ghostwriting for the CEO. One afternoon I was banging out an article, and I wrote a paragraph that stopped me cold. It stopped me because something new and very different had just showed up on the screen: my own voice. It's hard to explain, but the paragraph I'd just written resonated with something that had been sleeping all my life, something potent, something deep. I realised I could say things I cared about, and I could say them in a way no one else could. I stopped ghosting and started writing my own stuff.

But it was hard to write the sort of thing that gave me that same feeling. Where could I publish it? I would try to sneak some of myself into the articles I wrote for journals and magazines, but I usually had to disguise what I really wanted to say.

In 1995, I ended up in IBM's Internet division. A ranking PR guy from corporate headquarters ran into me one day and said he'd heard I had a lot of contacts in the financial press. He suggested we get together for lunch and talk about it. I took this as a good sign, maybe an opening to do what I liked best. But when we met several weeks later he said something like, 'All those journalists you know? Never talk to them again.'

He said I should refer all such conversations to him instead. That way, he said, the company's messaging would be consistent. Or words to that effect. But I knew they wouldn't be real conversations – they would be 'key message' pitches, and I wasn't about to subject people I knew and liked to that sort of targeting. I kept my contacts to myself.

I was devastated. It was bad enough that I'd been explicitly forbidden to speak with journalists, many of whom had become good friends, but where was I going to *write?* If I published anything, I'd get busted for not asking permission – there was that word again – and if I wrote sleazy PR for IBM, I'd have to kill myself to blot out the karmic stain.

And then it came to me: I could write on the World Wide Web! At that juncture, IBM's Internet division was so clueless I figured most of the top brass had only vaguely heard of it. One senior guy thought Yahoo was a kind of browser – no lie – and this was after the Yahoo IPO had made headlines in every major newspaper worldwide. Oh well, at least their PR was consistent.

I liked this idea. A lot. I'd be invisible on the Web, outside the control of any company. I'd be free at last to speak in my own voice without begging anyone's permission. I decided to create a Web-cum-e-mail newsletter. I wanted a catchy title, so I called it *Entropy Gradient Reversals*, EGR for short. In the beginning, I thought it would be a perfect vehicle to deliver my profound pundit-grade insights about the Internet and show everyone how smart I was. That didn't last long. I ended the very first issue like this:

> **From time to time we offer to share our list of subscribers with door-to-door aromatherapy salespersons and ritual ax-murderers. If you would prefer that your data not be used in this way, please check the box.**

Whoa! What a response that brought! Everyone was laughing. People subscribed in droves. I was ecstatic. I wondered whether IBM would have given me permission to publish such material. Probably not – on the off-chance of offending the aromatherapy and ritual ax-murderer market segments.

I started wondering what other sorts of noncorporate things I could write. What if I broke all the rules? You know, the unwritten rules everyone learns by telepathy at birth: be pleasant, be brief, don't speak down to your reader, don't use big words, don't use obscenity, don't make yourself the centre of attention. First and foremost, do that all-important market research. Find out what your audience wants to hear about. Ask their permission.

Wait a second … hadn't I been through all this? I had, and I'd had enough. I decided to go against the grain with a vengeance. I told readers they were clueless hosers. I interviewed an imaginary horse – at exhausting length. I used vocabulary so obscure that people needed unabridged dictionaries to figure out what I was saying. I developed an alter-ego named RageBoy®, a seriously maladjusted mental case and towering egomaniac with an advanced case of Tourette's syndrome. And my readers loved it.

Well … the ones who stayed loved it. Many went screaming for the nearest exit. RageBoy at full throttle is not everyone's cup of tea, to be sure. But the ones who stayed are an interesting lot. Some are programmers, teachers, artists, writers, full-time parents. Others have titles like Director of Public Relations, VP Marketing, Chief Information Officer, CEO. And the companies they come from read like the Fortune 500 list. The readership is not, as you might suspect, drawn from some dangerously misanthropic idiot fringe. The audience is regular people, mostly business people. And as the THX ads say: the audience is listening.

Forget my gonzo experimentation with RageBoy. That's just one microscopic example of what's happening online. The real point is that the Internet has made it possible for genuine human voices to be heard again, however different they may be from the cautious, insipid pabulum of mainstream broadcast media. Why has the Internet grown so rapidly? Why did it catch so many businesses off guard? The audience is listening because people are attracted to precisely the difference the Net provides: the sound of human beings talking with one another as human beings – the sound of a million conversations whose primary purpose, for once, is not to sell us something.

How do these conversations get started? How do people with common interests find each other? How does anyone find anything online? The simple answer is the theme of this book: word gets around. And on the Net, word gets around fast.

For every entry in the encyclopaedia, there is now a Web site. For any idea you can imagine – and some you can't – there are thousands of articles and images electronically swirling around the globe. But that's not the real story. That's not the big news. The word that's going around, the word that's finally getting out, is something much larger, far more fundamental. The word that's passing like a spark from keyboard to screen, from heart to mind, is the permission we're giving ourselves and each other: to be human and to speak as humans.

Consciously or not, millions of us are using the Internet to pass along this unconditional permission to millions of others. When enough people do that, something viral happens. It's not hypothetical, it's happening – when we say what we think, when we feel what we say, when we listen for the music of authentic presence. We are constantly searching each other out, linking, talking, shaking things up. Consciously or not, by the very nature of the permission we give each other, we are working to bring down business-as-usual.

News of this ever-spreading word is what you're reading here. And it's a little schizophrenic, I have to admit. In one sense, the news is good. It's great! It's the joyous noise of people revelling in a newfound freedom, laughing, jeering, cheering, irrepressible.

From another perspective, the news is not good at all. Everybody's miserable. Everybody's had about enough. People are sick to death of being valued only as potential buyers, as monetary grist for some modern-day satanic mill. They're sick of working for organisations that treat them as if they didn't exist, then attempt to sell them the very stuff they themselves produced. Why is a medium that holds such promise – to connect, to inspire, to awaken, to enlist, to change – being used by companies as a conduit for the kind of tired lies that have characterised 50 years of television? Business has made a ventriloquist's trick of the humanity we take for granted. The sham is ludicrous. The corporation pretends to speak, but its voice is that of a third-rate actor in a fourth-rate play, uttering lines no one believes in a manner no one respects.

Oh well. That's OK. We'll get by. We've got each other.

I have to laugh as I write that. The Internet audience is a strange crew, to be sure. But we're not talking about some Woodstock lovefest here. We don't all need to drop acid and get naked. We don't need to pledge our undying troth to each other, or to the Revolution, or to the bloody Cluetrain Manifesto for that matter. And neither does business.

All we need to do is what most of us who've discovered this medium are already doing: using it to connect with each other, not as representatives of corporations or market segments, but simply as who we are.

From hopelessly romantic meditations on favourite cats, to screeds so funny you'll blow coffee out of your nose, to collective code for alternative operating systems: we're all expressing ourselves in a new way online – a way that was never possible before, never before permitted. And make no mistake, speech once freed is a powerful drug. Get used to it; it ain't going back in the box. What does this mean for electronic commerce? Take a wild guess. We're not those neatly predictable consumers business remembers from yesterday. We got a taste of something else, and we like it. We'll make it ourselves, and defend it with a ferocity that might surprise most businesses. If you're a business, believe us: it's a surprise you'd just as soon skip. We're in the market for lots of things, but the market we see ourselves in is more like that ancient marketplace. Tell us some good stories and capture our interest. Don't talk to us as if you've forgotten how to speak. Don't make us feel small. Remind us to be larger. Get a little of that human touch.

People of earth …
Your choice is simple. Join us and live in peace
or pursue your present course and face obliteration.
We shall be waiting for your answer.
The decision rests with you.

The Day the Earth Stood Still (1951)

To find anything that isn't overtly complicit with the Great Technology Sitcom, you have to dig down to the underbelly of the Web. You have to get past the sites with commercial pretensions that are slicing and dicing you, counting the legs and dividing by four, bringing in the sheep. You are being incorporated into their demographic surveys. And, predictably, the lowest common denominator is getting all the juice. You are being packaged for advertisers by some of the hippest hucksters on the planet.

Dig deeper. Down to the sites that never entertained the hope of Buck One. They owe nobody anything. Not advertisers, not VC producers, not you. Put your ear to those tracks and listen to what's coming like a freight train. What you'll hear is the sound of passion unhinged, people who have had it up to here with white-bread culture, hooking up to form the biggest goddam garage band the world has ever seen.

What are these underbelly sites about? What's a rock concert about? How about creation, exploring a visceral and shared collective memory we've been brainwashed into believing never existed?

Conspiracy theory, my ass. Schools and teachers, the motor vehicle bureau, the IRS, the military, the line at the bank, the television set, the newspapers at the checkout stand, the news on your radio, the billboards along the highway, and now a hundred thousand cold-comfort Web sites. All are tuned to your brain at the deepest level and you have lined up for the coolest, latest-model implant. The carrier wave has been tuned at huge cost to deliver a single message: you are not free, you desire nothing but the products we produce, you have no world but the world we give you.

If you're OK with this, then eat it up. There's a bulimic's dream-feast of killer kontent on the way. But if it already makes you want to puke, get angry. Write it, code it, paint it, play it – rattle the cage however you can. Stay hungry. Stay free. And believe it: win, lose, or draw, we're here to stay. Armed only with imagination, we're gonna rip the fucking lid off.

There's your market.

Prospectus

OK, the scary part is over now. You can come out. It's safe.

In fact, the news gets better from here on in. And the first bit of news is that this isn't about us and them. It's about us. *Them* don't exist. Not really. Corporations are legal fictions, willing suspensions of disbelief. Pry the roof off any company and what do you find inside? The Crackerjack prize is ourselves, just ordinary people. We come in all flavours: funny, cantankerous, neurotic, compassionate, avaricious, generous, scheming, lackadaisical, brilliant, and a million other things. It's true that the higher up the food chain you go, the more likely you are to encounter the arrogant and self-deluded, but even top management types are mostly harmless when you get to know them. Given lots of love, some even make good pets.

Inside companies, outside companies, there are only people. All of us work for organisations of some sort, or we're peddling something. All of us pay the mortgage or the rent. We all buy shoes and books and food and time online, plus the occasional Beanie Baby for the kid. More important, all of us are finding our voices once again. Learning how to talk to one another. Slowly recovering from a near-fatal brush with zombification after watching Night of the Living Sponsor reruns all our lives.

Inside, outside, there's a conversation going on today that wasn't happening at all five years ago and hasn't been very much in evidence since the Industrial Revolution began. Now, spanning the planet via Internet and World Wide Web, this conversation is so vast, so multifaceted, that trying to figure what it's about is futile. It's about a billion years of pent-up hopes and fears and dreams coded in serpentine double helixes, the collective flashback déjà vu of our strange perplexing species. Something ancient, elemental, sacred, something very very funny that's broken loose in the pipes and wires of the 21st century.

There are millions of threads in this conversation, but at the beginning and end of each one is a human being. That this world is digital or electronic is not the point. What matters most is that it exists in narrative space. The story has come unbound. The world of commerce became precipitously permeable while it wasn't looking and sprang a leak from a quarter least expected. The dangers of democracy pale before the danger of uncontained life. Life with the wraps off. Life run wild.

Why do companies find this prospect terrifying? How, for instance, does the above description differ from the basic operation of a virgin forest? When he said, 'in wildness is the preservation of the world,' I bet Thoreau wasn't just thinking about old-growth trees. He also wrote a little ditty called *On Civil Disobedience*. There is a connection.

But don't look at us. For the defenceless position all you companies now find yourselves in, you can thank the creators of the Internet, the US Department of Defence. What a paradox. What a total hoot!

And you might as well hoot as cry about it. It's not the end of the world. It's the beginning of a new one. What's emerging is our story in the most fundamental sense, the human mythos weaving a vision of whatever it wants to become. There is no known deterrent. Take a deep breath, baby. Roll with it.

While this may sound spooky and mystical and terribly uncorporate, it isn't meant to put you Fortune 500 types off. When you get right down to it, human beings are spooky and mystical and terribly uncorporate, and corporations – if you'd only let yourselves admit it – consist entirely of human beings. Sort of neat how that works out. So the bottom line is: you can play in the Internet headspace as well as anyone.

There are just three conditions: 1) you have to let your people play for you, since there's really nobody else at home; 2) you have to play, not something more serious and goal-oriented; and 3) related to the previous, you have to have at least some tenuous notion of what 'headspace' might mean. It's not in the dictionary. But you can ask around. Get the general hang of the thing. If you figure it out, we'll think you're cool and consume mass quantities of all your wonderful products.

See how easy life can be when you loosen up a little?

You laugh, we laugh with you.

Either way, we live.

CHAPTER [2]

The longing

DAVID WEINBERGER

What is the Web for?

WE KNOW TELEPHONES ARE FOR TALKING with people, televisions are for watching programmes, and highways are for driving. So what's the Web for?

We don't know. Yet we put it on magazine covers, found businesses stoking it, spend billions on an infrastructure for it. We *want* it to be important with a desperation that can frighten us when we look at it coldly.

Who is this we? It's not just the webheads and full-time aficionados. It's the management teams who don't understand it but sense an opportunity. It's the uncles and aunts who pepper you with questions about all this Web stuff. It's the seven-year-old who takes it for granted that when she speaks the entire world can choose to hear her. Our culture's pulse is pounding with the Web.

This fervid desire for the Web bespeaks a longing so intense that it can only be understood as spiritual. A longing indicates that something is missing in our lives. What is missing is the sound of the human voice.

The spiritual lure of the Web is the promise of the return of voice.

Being managed

The longing for the Web occurs in the midst of a profoundly managed age.

We believe, in fact, that to be a business is to be managed. A business manages its resources, including its finances, physical plant and people in basically the same way: quantifiable factors are determined, predicted, processed, assessed.

But our management view extends far beyond business. We manage our households, our children, our wildlife, our ecological environment. And that which is unmanaged strikes us as bad: weeds, riots, cancer.

The idea that we can manage our world is uniquely 20th-century and chiefly American. And there are tremendous advantages to believing one lives in a managed world:

- **Risk avoidance.** Nothing unexpected happens if you're managing your world.

- **Smoothness.** Everything works in a managed environment simply because broken things are an embarrassment.

- Fairness. In earlier times, life was unfair. Now you're guaranteed your three-score and ten and if something 'goes wrong', the managed system will compensate you, even if you have to sue the bastards.

- **Discretionary attention.** If you were out in the wild, your attention would be drawn to every creaking twig and night howl. But now that the risks have been mitigated, things work right, and you can manage your time so you have not just leisure time but also discretionary attention: you can decide what interests you. Why, you can even have hobbies.

Of course, none of these benefits is delivered perfectly. There are still risks, there are still injustices, there are still 'outages'. But these are exceptions. And when they occur, we feel cheated, as if our contract has been violated.

It wasn't always thus. For millennia, we assumed that being in control was the exception and living in a wildly risk-filled world was the norm:

> As flies to wanton boys, are we to the gods.
> They kill us for their sport.
> **King Lear**

Today these awful words sound like one of those quaint, primitive ideas we've outgrown.

The belief in the managed environment is a denial of the brute 'facticity' of our lives. The truth is that businesses cannot be managed. They can be *run*, but they exist in a world that is so far beyond the control of the executives and the shareholders that 'managing' a business is a form of magical belief that gets punctured the first time a competitor drastically lowers prices, a large trading partner's economy falters, a key supplier's factory burns down, your lead developer gets a better offer, your CFO becomes felonious, or an angry consumer wins an unfair lawsuit.

As flies to wanton boys are companies to their markets. They pull off a company's wings for sport.

How to hate your job

A managed environment requires behaviour from us that we accept as inevitable although, of course, it is really mandatory only because it is mandated. We call it 'professionalism'.

Professionalism goes far beyond acting according to a canon of ethics. Professionals dress like other professionals (one eccentricity per person is permitted – a garish tie, perhaps, or a funky necklace), decorate their cubicles with nothing more disturbing than a Dilbert (formerly Far Side) cartoon, sit up straight at committee meetings, tell carefully calibrated jokes, don't undermine the authority of (that is, show they're smarter than) their superiors, make idle chatter only about a narrow range of 'safe' topics, don't swear, don't mention God, make absolutely no reference to being sexual (exceptions made for male executives after the hot new recruit has left the room), and successfully 'manage' their home life so that it never intrudes unexpectedly into their business life.

Most of us don't mind doing this. In fact, we actually sort of enjoy it. It's like playing grown-up. And having extremist political banners hung in cubicles or having to listen to someone talk about his spiritual commitments or sex life would simply be distracting. Disturbing, actually.

And yet … we feel resentment. Find someone who likes being managed, who feels fully at home in his or her professional self. Our longing for the Web is rooted in the deep resentment we feel towards being managed.

However much we long for the Web is how much we hate our job.

Our voice

Just about all the concessions we make to work in a well-run, non-disturbing, secure, predictably successful, managed environment have to do with giving up our voice.

Nothing is more intimately a part of who we are than our voice. It expresses what we think and feel. It is an amalgam of the voluntary and involuntary. It gives style and shape to content. It subtends the most public and the most private. It is what we withhold at the moments of greatest significance.

Our voice is our strongest, most direct expression of who we are. Our voice is expressed in our words, our tone, our body language, our visible enthusiasms.

Our business voice – in a managed environment – is virtually the same as everyone else's. For example, we learn to write memos in The Standard Style and to participate in committee meetings in The Appropriate Fashion. (Of course, we are also finely attuned to minute differences in expression and can often tell memos apart the way birdwatchers spot the differences between a lark sparrow and a song sparrow.)

In 50 years, our corporate lives will seem no different than those of the 1950s. Whether we are Ward Cleavers or Dilberts, we all reported to work in look-alike rooms, wearing uniforms, speaking civilly, playing our parts at committee meetings. The fact that earth tones and Rockports have replaced grey flannel and wingtips isn't going to separate us from our crewcut fathers.

Managed businesses have taken our voices. We want to struggle against this. We wear a snarky expression behind our boss's back, place ironic distance between our company and ourselves, and we don't want to think we have become our parents. But we have. And we've done so willingly.

Management is a powerful force, part of a larger life-scheme that promises us health, peace, prosperity, calm and no surprises in every aspect of our lives, from health to wealth to good weather and moderately heated coffee from McDonald's. We are all victims of this assault on voice, the attempt to get us to shut up and listen to the narrowest range of ideas imaginable.

It is only the force of our regret at having lived in this bargain that explains the power of our longing for the Web.

The longing

We don't know what the Web is for but we've adopted it faster than any technology since fire.

There are many ways to look at what's drawing us to the Web: access to information, connection to other people, entrance to communities, the ability to broadcast ideas. None of these are wrong perspectives. But they all come back to the promise of voice and thus of authentic self.

At the first InternetWorld conference, the vendors were falling over one another offering software and services that would let you 'create your own home page in five minutes'. Microsoft, IBM and a hundred smaller shops were all hawking the same goods. You could sit in a booth and create your own home page faster than you can get your portrait sketched on a San Francisco sidewalk.

While the create-a-home-page problem proved too easy to solve to support a software industry, there was something canny about the commercial focus on the creation of home pages. Since you could just as adequately view the Web as a huge reference library, why did home pages seize our imaginations? Because a home page is a place in which we can express who we are and let the world in. Meagre though it may be, a home page is a way of having a voice.

The Web's promise of a voice has now gone far beyond that. The Web is viral. It infects everything it touches – and, because it is an airborne virus, it infects some things it doesn't. The Web has become the new corporate infrastructure, in the form of intranets, turning massive corporate hierarchical systems into collections of many small pieces loosely joining themselves unpredictably.

The voice that the Web gives us is not the ability to post pictures of our cat and our guesses at how the next episode of The X-Files will end. It is the granting of a place in which we can be who we are (and even who we aren't, if that's the voice we've chosen).

It is a public place. That is crucial. Having a voice doesn't mean being able to sing in the shower. It means presenting oneself to others. The Web provides a place like we've never seen before.

We may still have to behave properly in committee meetings, but increasingly the real work of the company is getting done by quirky individuals who meet on the Web, net the two-hour committee meeting down to two lines (one of which is obscene and the other wickedly funny), and then – in a language and rhythm unique to them – move ahead faster than the speed of management.

The memo is dead. Long live e-mail. The corporate newsletter is dead. Long live racks of 'zines from individuals who do not speak for the company. Bland, safe relationships with customers are dead. Long live customer-support reps who are willing to get as pissed off at their own company as the angry customer is.

We are so desperate to have our voices back that we are willing to leap into the void. We embrace the Web not knowing what it is, but hoping that it will burn the organisation chart – if not the organisation – down to the ground. Released from the grey-flannel handcuffs, we say anything, curse like sailors, rhyme like bad poets, flame against our own values, just for the pure delight of having a voice.

And when the thrill of hearing ourselves speak again wears off, we will begin to build a new world.

That is what the Web is for.

Make a bonfire of your reputations

When I was asked to make this address I wondered what I had to say to you boys who are graduating. And I think I have one thing to say. If you wish to be useful, never take a course that will silence you. Refuse to learn anything that implies collusion, whether it be a clerkship or a curacy, a legal fee or a post in a university. Retain the power of speech no matter what other power you may lose. If you can take this course, and in so far as you take it, you will bless this country. In so far as you depart from this course you become dampers, mutes, and hooded executioners.

As a practical matter a mere failure to speak out upon occasions where no opinion is asked or expected of you, and when the utterance of an uncalled-for suspicion is odious, will often hold you to a concurrence in palpable iniquity. Try to raise a voice that will be heard from here to Albany and watch what comes forward to shut off the sound. It is not a German sergeant, nor a Russian officer of the precinct. It is a note from a friend of your father's offering you a place in his office. This is your warning from the secret police. Why, if any of you young gentleman have a mind to make himself heard a mile off, you must make a bonfire of your reputations and a close enemy of most men who would wish you well.

I have seen ten years of young men who rush out into the world with their messages, and when they find how deaf the world is, they think they must save their strength and wait. They believe that after a while they will be able to get up on some little eminence from which they can make themselves heard. 'In a few years,' reasons one of them, 'I shall have gained a standing, and then I will use my powers for good.' Next year comes and with it a strange discovery. The man has lost his horizon of thought. His ambition has evaporated; he has nothing to say. I give you this one rule of conduct. Do what you will, but speak out always. Be shunned, be hated, be ridiculed, be scared, be in doubt, but don't be gagged. The time of trial is always. Now is the appointed time.

– John Jay Chapman
Commencement address to the graduating class, Hobart College, 1900

C H A P T E R [3]

Talk is cheap

RICK LEVINE

The voice emerges literally from the body
as a representation of our inner world.
It carries our experience from the past,
our hopes and fears for the future,
and the emotional resonance of the moment.
If it carries none of these, it must be
a masked voice, and having muted the voice,
anyone listening knows intuitively
we are not all there.

David Whyte, *The Heart Aroused*

Voices from pots

I'M A POTTER'S KID. When I was growing up, we always had red-brown carpet and rugs to help hide the terracotta dust we tracked home from Dad's shop. I have fond memories of watching Italian potters with doorway-wide shoulders spin clay into forms larger than myself, effortlessly raising planters, lamps, bowls and jars from undistinguished lumps of mud, one after the other, parading dozens of seemingly identical forms across the studio floor. Whenever I see a large thrown shape, I remember the first time I tried to throw 25 pounds of clay, thinking I would start with less than the 60 or 70 pounds I saw growing like graceful mushrooms on my dad's wheels. I landed flat on my back, shoulder blades bruised, smelling 20 years of clay dust on the wood floor beneath my head, as the misshapen lump of clay took advantage of my first indecision, knocking me from the wheel and covering the studio wall in red mud. You can't learn to throw large forms without losing lots of them in the process.

Pots are made by people. Large ones especially remind me of that human authorship. Smaller things – mugs, cups, pitchers – touch me as well. They're fitted to a potter's hands, reflecting their measure. I can gauge the size of the artisans' hands, the length of their fingers, from lips, spouts and pulled handles. There's so much more life invested in a thrown piece than in anonymous cast or stamped ware. A medium such as clay, elevated and transformed by human shaping, bears witness to the life that moulded it into something more than plain stuff.

When experienced potters describe their craft, they often talk about seeing the form they're creating in their mind's eye, applying force to make the spinning clay match its virtual, internal archetype. There's an incredible amount of practice, failure and learning that has to take place before we develop the courage and surety to trust such an internal, private muse, to ignore the contrary opinions of others and do what we know will succeed.

Despite too many years spent behind keyboards and display screens building software, creating Web sites, and generally using technology more than is good for me, I'm still a potter's kid. I consider myself an artist and a craftsman, and bring a craftsman's attitudes to my work and life. One perspective that seems to surface with some regularity is a deeply instilled obligation to do new work, create stuff people have never seen before. It's a peculiar approach to life, picked up mostly by osmosis at some early age from my parents and relatives. In execution, it's a standard requiring constant exploration and reinvention, but also a certain studied ignorance of what's considered right and proper. There's a bit of irrationality in believing that if I follow my own intuition and, at some level, don't pay attention to what other people think, I'll create unique works that will surprise and delight.

Artists have a stubborn faith in their ability to create newness from next to nothing. This faith shapes their work, enables them to establish themselves as individuals, fingerprinting their way through their medium.

What's this got to do with business? With organisations? Lots. Most of the creative people and knowledge workers organisations depend on, those whose sense of self-worth is centered in the pride they take in the work of their heads and hands, will have an immediate 'been there, done that' reaction to this description of artistic identity. From the electronic pressroom gang, to the MIS boiler-room toilers to the hackers building an insurance-entitlement management application to increase next year's sales – all have some of the attitude of the craftsman. People in high tech take pride in their work. They are individuals who see the details of the things they produce in the light of the trials and triumphs they experience while creating products. In the courage of creation, they find a place to hang their individuality. Programmers and techno types appreciate elegant, spare code and the occasional well-turned architectural hack. My accountant friends get off on clever spreadsheet macros, and on being able to slant this quarter's results to shade meaning within the arcane constraints of the law. Even managers leave their telltale fingerprints on their jobs – the well-coached team rising to unexpected heights, or the business relationship blossoming into a long-term sales annuity. Some people apply a craftsmanlike care to their work and their voices are heard, remarked upon, and recognised as uniquely theirs.

> Claude Levi-Strauss, the French anthropologist, discusses *bricolage* as the opportunism of those who work with their hands, creating stuff out of whatever is lying about. The Web is group bricolage. Individuals build it without working from a master plan. They take pieces that work – stealing gifs, formats, links – and create new pages. This makes the Web unpredictable, creative and always the result of human hands.
> – David Weinberger

The Web is no different. Every Web page we see has a person behind it. Sometimes their individual decisions are eroded and digested by being passed through a corporate colon of editors, gatekeepers and other factota, but there are clear signposts to individual care and concern on much of today's Web. While all print and broadcast media have at least some indirect personal authorship, there's a key difference on the Web. The percentage of 'raw' content published, direct from a creator's fingers to our eyes, is much higher than in traditional media. The Web's low cost of entry to publishers, both small and large, and the amount of unfiltered chat/newsgroup/e-mail text finding its way into search engines guarantees our daily browsing experience has a very strong flavour of individual authorship.

> **R**ick may believe he's good at multitasking, but I don't believe It. Humans can't multitask – we can't pay attention to two things simultaneously.
>
> You can multitask? Fine. then read a book and write one at the same time. No, multitasking is really just rapid attention-switching. And that'd be a useful skill, except it takes us a second or two to engage in the new situation we've graced with our focus. So, the sum total of attention is actually decreased as we multitask. Slicing your attention, in other words, is less like slicing potatoes than like slicing plums: you always lose some of the juice.
>
> – David Weinberger

Inevitably, our heightened awareness of distinct, individual voices engenders the urge to talk back, to engage, to converse. The software and mechanisms developed helter-skelter for the Net cater to these urges. Chat, free e-mail, automatic home pages – all reinforce our feeling that not only is it easy to enter into discourse with others, but also that we're by-god *entitled* to wade into the conversational stream. Heaven help you if you get in my way, or try to stifle my voice.

The good or bad news, depending on your perspective, is that it's hard to fake your end of one of these conversations. Ever been on the phone with a friend or co-worker while sitting in front of a computer and trying to read or respond to e-mail when your wire addiction gets the better of you? I'm very good at multitasking, and can fool many people some of the time, but I get caught more often than I'll admit. (By my wife, for instance. Every time.) We can tell when someone is engaged, listening, responding honestly, and with his or her full faculties. We're wired to interpret subtle clues telling us whether a person is all there, if we're the centre of their attention, if we're being heard. No matter how starved for detail our communication channel, our brains manage to get a gestalt reading on the other party's presence.

In the same way we distinguish personal attention from inattention, we can tell the difference between a commercial pitch and words that come when someone's life animates their message. Try snipping paragraphs of text from press releases and a few pieces of printed person-to-person e-mail. Shuffle the paper slips. Hand the pile to your office-mate, your spouse or your next-door neighbour. Can they sort them? Of course they can, in short order. People channel from their hearts directly to their words. That's voice. It comes of focus, attention, caring, connection and honesty of purpose. It is not commercially motivated, isn't talk with a vested interest. Talk is cheap. The value of our voices is beyond mere words. The human voice reaches directly into our beings and touches our spirits.

Voice is how we can tell the difference between people, committees and bots. An e-mail written by one person bears the tool marks of their thought processes. E-mail might be employee-to-employee, customer-to-customer or employee-to-customer, but in each case it's person-to-person. Voice, or its lack, is how we tell what's worth reading and what's not. Much of what passes for communication from companies to customers is washed and diluted so many times by the successive editing and tuning done by each company gatekeeper that the live-person hints are lost.

Authenticity, honesty and personal voice underlie much of what's successful on the Web. Its egalitarian nature is engendering a renaissance in personal publishing. We of genus Homo are wired to respond to each other's noise and commotion, to the rich, multi-modal deluge of data each of us broadcasts as we wade through life. The Web gives us an opportunity to escape from the bounds imposed by broadcast media's one-to-many notions of publishing. Nascent Web publishing efforts have their genesis in a burning need to say something, but their ultimate success comes from people wanting to listen, needing to hear each other's voices, and answering in kind.

Wired conversations

The message here isn't new and isn't particularly complex. Our elevator pitch is a pretty short one:

> People talk to each other. In open, straightforward conversations. Inside and
> outside organisations. The inside and outside conversations are connecting.
> We have no choice but to participate in them.

If there's any newness, it's in how the Net and the Web change the balance of the conversational equation. Technology is putting a sharper, more urgent point on the importance of conversation. Conversations are moving faster, touching more people and bridging greater distances than we're used to. Let's take a tour of the various conversational modalities the Net offers and how they carry our voices.

E-mail

Electronic mail is the wedge cracking the rock of corporate communication. I write a message, label it with **yourname@wherever_you_are.com**, click the 'send' button, and you've got my mail. Most corporate electronic defences pass it right through. They might screen out applets, viruses and other denizens of the internetworked dark, but words slip through like wraiths. Thoughts. Ideas. Kudos. Complaints. Jokes. We exchange the mundane, day-to-day electronic utterances greasing our business down its intended path. We also trade other missives, possibly words my management would rather I didn't speak, or didn't hear. But the flow can't be stopped, not without choking off the lifeblood of most businesses. The inexpedient comes with the expedient, and we have no choice but to work with it. The basic operating rule of e-mail is that anyone can send mail to almost anyone else – all they need is an address.

E-mail is a more immediate medium than paper. My expectation of the response time to many messages I send is today, not tomorrow or a week from now. This urgency means I'm more apt to write quickly and conversationally when I respond to a message. A lot of the spontaneity in e-mail messages comes from writers breaking through their natural caution and reserve, rushing the writing process, giving themselves permission to be blunt, honest and sincere in response to a query. It's not just a question of knowing how to type, but of giving myself permission to truly converse: to 'out' myself in a conversational medium that is informal, honest, yet open to myriad misinterpretations if I choose words and phrases carelessly. Despite this scary thought, most people don't find person-to-person e-mail daunting. The ease and directness of e-mail is forging new connections – new conversations – throughout virtually every business. Type-click-deliver.

Mailing lists

Mailing lists come in two basic flavours, one-way and two-way. One-way lists let me send to a large number of people at once, but recipients can't respond to the entire list the message was sent to. There's no opportunity for conversation, other than between you, the recipient, and me, the list owner. These lists can often have the character of a mass mailing, like a Christmas card list. If the mailing is from someone you don't know who's trying to sell you something, convince you of something, or lure you to a particular Web site, it's called *spam*.

There's a fascinating subgenus of the one-way list called a webzine or an e-zine, as in electronic magazine. These are periodic bouts of creative journalism sent to willing subscribers, with audiences ranging from dozens to hundreds of thousands. To their devotees, they have all the interest and attraction of their well-funded offline counterparts. However, they're often more focused, more idiosyncratic, and less plastic. They're usually created in someone's garage or bedroom office as a labour of love given a pulpit by the incredibly low entry cost of Internet publishing. They may start out like the *Utne Reader* or *Mother Jones* magazine, but the Web relieves them of the need to raise capital, rent a press and pay for postage. Many 'zines have a strong conversational tone. They mine the incoming stream of responses to take the temperature of their constituencies, and relay tasty bits back to their audiences. The conversation this engenders often feels like publishing with a more immediate feedback loop.

Two-way lists are even more interesting from a conversational viewpoint. They let recipients respond to messages, and everyone else on the list sees their responses. But it takes time to wade through all the traffic on a busy list, sifting value from chaff, knowledge from data. As individual mailing lists grow from small, focused forums, they can easily turn into large, unwieldy free-for-alls. The commitment required to understand the content and context of a list before you post to it is part of the conversational ante this aspect of the Net requires. Just like voice conversations, these asynchronous exchanges reveal if you're all there, focused and paying attention.

In a moderated two-way list, all mail to the list is screened by someone doing gatekeeper duty. The moderator's role ranges from that of a friendly guide to being an editor with absolute control over every message sent to the list. Moderators often end up having a great deal of influence on the tenor and substance of list conversations.

Conversations on two-way lists look just like conversations in personal e-mail, except the odds of having several people responding independently to the same piece of mail go way up. The conversation may branch, spawn side discussions, and loop back on itself as each new person throws in her or his two cents.

Newsgroups

Newsgroups are similar to mailing lists, except messages collect on special computers on the Internet configured as 'news servers'. (A business can also have news servers for internal company discussions, not available on the pubic Internet.) I can point a newsreader at the server to check in when I want to, rather than seeing all the messages accumulate in my e-mail in-box, willy-nilly. Newsgroups can be either moderated or unmoderated, just like mailing lists. Newsgroups also record the conversational thread structure of their messages, unlike e-mail, so you can see who is talking to whom and why.

The information space encompassed by publicly available newsgroups, called Usenet, is enormous. Every month, millions of conversations across the globe are enabled by newsgroups. Where e-mail conversations are often between people who know one another, Usenet exchanges are often between strangers. It's a medium that encourages discourse, and can create a kind of community among its participants.

All of these channels for conversation – e-mail, mailing lists, newsgroups – begin to look more alike as you use them. At some point, you start paying more attention to the messages and conversations, and less to the differences in software and tools employed by the various electronic delivery channels.

For our purposes, the biggest difference between electronic and paper mail is the ease with which a single message can be distributed to a vast audience, and then serve as a seed for conversation. I can forward your mail to my friends. To lots of my friends.

To lots of people I've never met before, but who might be very interested in what you have to say about your company's management, policies or practices. I can do this on a scale far exceeding paper distribution. And I can do it before lunch.

Here's a real-life example of how a conversation ignores the boundaries between companies and their customers. It starts with a posting to a newsgroup for Saturn car owners, rec.autos.makers.saturn, an entirely reasonable question about how much service should cost and how much control a car owner has over what gets done to his car. This newsgroup isn't owned or in any way managed by Saturn. It's just ordinary people, talking about their cars.[1]

> Subject:
> Am I Getting F-'ed By My Saturn Dealer???
> Date: 1999/06/29
> Author: Ross <rossxxx@xxx.com>
>
> **I would like to hear you'alls opinions and experiences. I got a 99 SC2 with now 17k. My owners manual says at 9k and 15k all it needs is an oil change.**
>
> **At 9k I got charged $50 and they tacked on a 9k Service card that says: Oil Change, Top Off Fluids, check and adjust tires, check all lights in & out, inspect brakes, inspect throttle linkage, lube door & hood hinges.**
>
> **At 15k I got charged $113 and they tacked on a 15k Service card that says: Oil Change, Top Off Fluids, check and adjust tires, check all lights in & out, inspect brakes, inspect throttle linkage, lube door & hood hinges, inspect cooling system, clean engine, test onboard computer, report tire wear.**
>
> **Now I recognize that doing that kind of work requires some payment, BUT all I was expecting them to do (and me to pay for) was only an Oil Change. What gives?? At what point of ownership do I get what service Saturn requires as opposed to what my Saturn Dealer requires, and why is there a difference?**
>
> **Comments are most appreciated especially from the Techs!!**
>
> **Thanks...............Ross**

I've shortened this sequence from its original length of about 20 messages, and edited individual messages to save us some reading time. I've also disguised people's names and e-mail addresses, to protect their privacy.

Someone chimes in about how much similar service costs them – customers of two vendors comparing notes, from the comfort of their home or office:

> Subject: Re:
> Am I Getting F-'ed By My Saturn Dealer???
> Date: 1999/06/29
>
> **Author: ranger_xxx <ranger_xxx@xxx.xxx.com>**
> **Where are you taking your car for service? Those prices sound high. At the**
> **store I go, the 9k and 15k are just oil changes and the charge is less than**
> **$27. I'd shop around other nearby Saturn stores and see what they charge.**

Then, some tips for getting along with your car dealer – reference information and advice, a testimonial in support of Saturn dealers:

> Subject: Re:
> Am I Getting F-'ed By My Saturn Dealer???
> Date: 1999/06/29
>
> **Author: Eric <eric@xx.xx.xxxx.com>**
> **You do have the right to bring your car in at any of these intervals and**
> **request that ONLY an oil change be done. If that's what you requested and**
> **that's not what they did then I would have a discussion with the service**
> **manager and just tell him that you requested only an oil change, you know**
> **they recommended more work, but didn't want that, and see what they say.**
> **Every service manager I've talked to in about 8 different shops has always**
> **been very helpful and appreciates it when these things are brought to their**
> **attention.**
>
> **Eric**
> **94 SL2 HCS**

So far, so good, but here's a pointer to another car dealer's service price list. If I were a slightly shady service manager, I'd worry, as my customers have gone beyond anecdotal comparisons to posting real prices. Now it's harder to lie with a straight face. And exposure isn't limited to the dozen or so people who posted to this discussion, but extends to thousands who might search for 'saturn customer service' and find this thread:

Subject: Re:
Am I Getting F-'ed By My Saturn Dealer???
Date: 1999/06/29
Author: Al xxx<axxx@xxx.net>

Ross,
Here is the URL for the Retailers in Columbus, Ohio and what THEY
recommend. It has additions to what the Owner's Handbook says but they
typically let me choose to do or not to do the EXTRA items.

Hope this helps!
Al

Some comic relief from the peanut gallery …

Subject: Re:
Am I Getting F-'ed By My Saturn Dealer???
Date: 1999/06/29
Author: newxxx <jasonxxx@xxx.com>

YOU WERE HAD!!!!
SUE SUE SUE

More disgruntlement. No one from the dealership being flamed answered this post.
Some readers will assume this omission validates the indictment of Saturn's
service, and the company will lose business. Further, since Saturn corporate minions
didn't wade into the discussion at this point, Saturn may have lost some
prospective customers.

Subject: Re:
Am I Getting F-'ed By My Saturn Dealer???
Date: 1999/06/30
Author: Leexx <leexx@xxx.net>

Midtown Saturn in Toronto does the same thing. $177 for the 60,000 KM
service. When I pointed out to the service rep that the Saturn manual didn't
call for coolant change etc. they had to check with service manager only to
agree to not change coolant (as if car owner's words are not to be trusted).
When I picked up the car, instead of charging me for the usual $30 oil
change, they simply subtracted the cost of coolant change ($90) from $177.

And they also charged me half an hour labor for inspecting vibrating brakes and noisy steering which was supposed to be covered under warranty.

The end result was a $145 oil change. And the car was washed, but not clean as there were many dusty missed spots. To add insult to injury, they won't drive me to pick up the car because I arranged the pick up only with the driver, not the service rep. So add another $25 cab ride.

Even though Saturn makes good cars for the price and sales reps are nice, some dealer's service dept needs to catch up to the rest of the corporation.

I'll NEVER GO TO TORONTO MIDTOWN SATURN again and encourage everyone else to boycott them.

I'm buying another new car in 18 months (wife and I each get new cars every 3 years). This bad experience will certainly be a factor. It's too bad other nice Saturn dealers will lose out because of this one dealer.

Now, a different sort of animal. This is a response from a Saturn employee, a technician, explaining how the game is played. This is an after-hours posting from a real person, and may or may not have been sanctioned by Saturn. This represents the firewall bleed-through at the heart of the Cluetrain Manifesto: honest comments from employees, unfiltered, going directly to customers.

Subject: Re:
Am I Getting F-'ed By My Saturn Dealer???
Date: 1999/06/30
Author: Bluexxx <bluexxx@xxx.com>

>At what point of ownership do I get what

>service Saturn requires as opposed to what

>my Saturn Dealer requires, and why is

>there a difference?

>Comments are most appreciated especially

>from the Techs!!

Its late for me after a 12 hour Saturn day but I will give a brief answer. If you want a real detailed answer feel free to ask more questions.

Saturn Corp. issues its 'recommended ' services and intervals. For warranty purposes these are all you need to follow as far as maintenance goes. Saturn

Dealers, on the other hand, are free to amend them in pretty much what ever way they want, intervals and price included.

I have worked at 2 different dealers. My current one is much smaller and the prices are much cheaper. There is a $15 difference in labour rate and the dealers are only 1.5 hrs apart. The items included in each service are somewhat different but not as drastic as yours. I have seen dealers include an alignment with every 12k. I have seen cooling services done at 24k. Lots of variations. I don't personally like it because when you get cars from other dealers they are out of sync.

I asked Saturn Corp. why they don't mandate a stricter policy towards service intervals. They said its illegal for them to force

a dealer to do that.

I hope this helps a little. Feel free to ask any question you have. I personally agree that what happened to you sucks. Our dealer the 9k and 15 k are oil changes at about $22.

And, in this case, our Net fairy godmother has the last word. Truth, justice, and a testimonial to the power of the Net. Right.

Subject: Re:
Am I Getting F-'ed By My Saturn Dealer???—UPDATE
Date: 1999/07/14
Author: Ross <ross@xxx.com>

My Saturn Dealer agreed I was getting F'ed. AND 'in an effort to earn your trust we extend a free 18k service.' So I took them up on it and spoke to the guy in charge (since he didn't respond to my e-mail). He said that the Dealer is 'rethinking' its 15k service. I guess between these posts and my response to Saturn's 15k service inquiry, they got the message. So, I guess I'm almost even and at 21k will ask for a simple oil change.

Ross

This conversation wasn't simply a business correspondence. It was among lots of people, ordinary folks. These people are writing in their own voices because they want to talk, to help, to contribute. If it's not altruism, it's something close to it – with maybe an occasional touch of revenge. We listen to their voices to decide whom to trust, and we can come to some pretty accurate conclusions about who's on the mark and who's full of hot air.

There's even overt comic relief and some entertainment. We listen carefully to what wasn't said, and who didn't participate in the conversation. The Saturn dealers are conspicuous by their absence. Their silence speaks as loudly as their words might have, had they joined in. The Saturn mechanic was speaking for his company in a new way: honestly, openly, probably without his boss's explicit sanction. He gave away secrets, took a risk, was humanised – and he greatly served the interests of Saturn. He and others like him are changing the way Saturn supports its customers. And Saturn corporate might not even know it's happening.

This puts a completely different spin on 'talk is cheap'. The mechanic's e-mail didn't cost Saturn a nickel. He wrote it on his own time. Companies need to harness this sort of caring and let its viral enthusiasm be communicated in employees' own voices. Pay a little, get a lot. Talk is cheap.

Technology is making these conversational needles a lot easier to find in the Internet haystack. There are search services anyone can use to find this stuff. General purpose newsgroup searchers like deja.com keep conversations like these online for varying lengths of time. Some for a very long time. The Internet has a wonderfully retentive memory, and we're constantly working to make it easier to retrieve little-used trivia from its magnetic depths. Don't bet against customers' ability to type your organisation's equivalent of 'lousy saturn customer service' into their favourite search engine and see your latest ugly truth displayed on their computer screen. And they'll chime in and tell their story. Your story.

Chat

Chat gets a bad rap. The Web canard says all chat sessions degenerate into conversations about sex within five minutes. It ain't so. Because it is immediate – taking place in real time – chat can enable conversation that feels more genuine, more substantial, and more human than any other Net channel.

The aspect of chat that still amazes me is that it can compress distance, enabling globe-spanning conversation in a visceral, obvious way. E-mail can connect people over the same distances, but it doesn't trigger the sense of wonder I experience when I see words appearing on my screen typed live by someone half a world away. Here's a snippet of chat conversation between two friends. The chat session was set up following an international artists workshop held in Tblisi, Georgia, and ran for several months. Belt is in London, Annie in Tblisi.

Belt:–*Just Entered The Room*–

Belt: **hello is anyone there?**

Belt: **its Belt here ... waiting for a full gas bottle so I can get warm ...**

Annie:–*Just Entered The Room*–

Belt: **drinking tea, wondering how to make a living ... (london transport has just gone up again! £3.80 for a travel card now ... don't know how people manage it!)**

Annie: **50 tetri in Tbilisi hey?**

Belt: **crazy, ... what do you think of the euro? and custard pies!!**

Annie: **I guess theres no difference in some way ... is it cold in London?**

Belt: **well its not so cold, just dark ... how about there? are you still snowed in?**

Annie: **whats that about ... over here its snowstorms deep snow, ploughs the airports shutdown**

Belt: **will you be able to get back?**

Annie: **spending time face up to snow flakes lying in bed of white sparkly comfort ... making snow angels ... have you ever made a snow angel? ... tis all new to me**

Belt: **I remember making snow angels on dartmoor, face up to the sky lying on the cold ground ...**

Annie: **I hope to fly Thurs get in Friday ... but apparently theres another storm on the way ... its incredibly beautiful, esp. on the industrial landscape of the lake (which looks like the sea ... huge)**

Belt: **it was like trying to fall off the earth ... sounds incredible ... immense landscapes. I haven't seen the sky since Mirzaani**

http://www.devoid.demon.co.uk/generator/chat4.htm

One definition of community is a group of people who care about each other more than they have to. This isn't a business exchange, even remotely. It is conversation, the verbal glue binding people separated by geography into a community. Chat's important to us corporate types because it's a medium where it's almost impossible to operate within the old rules. Because chat is a 'live' medium, there's little leeway for faking a voice, for a sophist approximation of a person. You can adopt a new persona, but you're going to need to button it all the way up and live it, or we'll be able to tell there's someone else underneath. Chat is CB radio on steroids. It's immediate and unwashed. If you can't type and think at the same time, you're in deep weeds. We can't broadcast, can't message, can't spew corporate pabulum in a chat environment. If business could successfully integrate chat into its marketing universe, companies would be on their way to shaking off some of the mass-media shackles separating them from customers.

One of the more interesting uses of a chat service has been to provide live customer support for Web sites without resorting to expensive telephone call centres. Liveperson.com is selling a service using a pop-up chat client connected to a 24/7 call centre to provide live, on-the-spot support to Web customers. Each support rep can field up to four simultaneous chat sessions. Customers get an immediate, interactive support person to answer their questions.

> Constantin: **Hi there, rick. What can I help you with today?**
>
> rick: **Hi Constantin. Could you tell me if your service can work with query string tokens instead of cookies?**
>
> Constantin: **Can I just clarify what you are asking … are you looking to track users using querystrings?**
>
> rick: **No, I need a solution that works even if a person refuses to accept cookies, or if their firewall/browser rejects cookies.**
>
> Constantin: **or are you referring to being a user and receiving a cookie when you begin to chat?**
>
> rick: **Yep.**
>
> Constantin: **If you hold on one second I can find out for you …**
>
> rick: **Great. Thanks.**
>
> Constantin: **I'm sorry but it is not possible right now to offer the service without sending cookies**

rick: **Ah. Is it planned?**

Constantin: **Just a moment please ...**

Constantin: **Not at the present time.**

rick: **Ok. Thanks for taking the time.**

Constantin: **Thanks for visiting.**

There's none of the hit-or-miss multiday waiting we get with e-mail support, no phone cost to the customer or vendor. Commerce sites have reportedly been experiencing dramatically increased sales from the high-touch attention they can give their customers.

Web pages

The Web lets us look into other people's lives in an intimate way. It enables us to see people as they are, close up. Have you ever been browsing for information, read an interesting page, followed the author's name link, and tripped through his personal pages, read his badly written poetry, looked at pictures of his dog, cat, family, friends and trip to the Bahamas?

For instance, while browsing slashdot.org, I read a comment from Chris Worth, followed a breadcrumb trail to **www.chrisworth.com** and was captivated by his personal Web phantasmagoria – including a cogent comparison of users of Microsoft productivity tools to frogs in pots of

Chat forces us to be human and fully present. Except for those of us who start out as gorillas ...

HaloMyBaby: **Welcome, Dr. Patterson and Koko, we're so happy you're here!**

DrPPatrsn: **You're welcome!**

HaloMyBaby: **Is Koko aware that she's chatting with thousands of people now?**

LiveKOKO: **Good here.**

DrPPatrsn: **Koko is aware.**

HaloMyBaby: **I'll start taking questions from the audience now, our first question is: MInyKitty asks Koko are you going to have a baby in the future?**

LiveKOKO: **Pink**

DrPPatrsn: **We've had earlier discussion about colors today**

LiveKOKO: **Listen, Koko loves eat**

HaloMyBaby: **Me too!**

DrPPatrsn: **What about a baby? She's thinking...**

LiveKOKO: **Unattention**

DrPPatrsn: **She covered her face with her hands.... which means it's not happening, basically, or it hasn't happened yet.**

LiveKOKO: **I don't see it.**

http://www.envirolink.org/ kokotranscript.html

No, I didn't make it up! Worried about 800-pound media gorillas dominating the Net?

heating water, and a scary little piece about his view of helicopters. Another time, I searched for how-to information about a software program I was installing, found an article written by Glenn Fleishman, clicked on his byline link to **www.glenns.org** and was engrossed in his story of how he fought Hodgkin's disease and won.

I do this frequently. In my mind's eye, I watch myself clicking off my intended path, wondering what the draw is, why I am allowing myself to be diverted from my goal. It's because I enjoy listening to people. They give me windows into their lives, providing substance as a foil to the superficial factual gloss of their day jobs. I'm seduced into spending time staring at evidence of their humanity, despite my better judgment against such a 'waste of time'. And then I do it again. And again.

> Early on in Sun's exploration of the Web, our best site efforts came from small teams with broad skills who didn't have too many constraints placed on what they were supposed to create. They had to work quickly and invent solutions to problems nobody had ever faced before. Perhaps because of the variety of skills the teams had to integrate and the short time lines, customers said they thought the sites looked like the result of people having fun and moving quickly. We never had the time to 'corporatise' them.

The fact that Web pages are conversations hasn't sunk in because they look like publications. But they are conversations: expressions of individual voices looking for a response. The Web pages we revisit often have feedback mechanisms and change over time in response to that feedback. Further, they must change visibly or people won't come back. We expect change, reaction, reflection of our comments and feedback. This is not just true with respect to personal Web pages. There's a very strong desire for corporate Web pages to have a human feel – to speak to us in some genuine way. This desire cries out for communication that's less formal, less professional, less anonymous, and more for the people reading than for the company doing the writing.

Hart Scientific, Inc. (**www.hartscientific.com**) posted a convenient comparison of conversational versus traditional writing on their Web site. They have two versions of their Y2K compliance page. You can tell them apart:

> Noncompliance issues could arise if Hart Scientific manufactured products are combined with other manufacturer's products. Hart cannot test all possible system configurations in which Hart manufactured products could be incorporated. Our products currently test as being compliant and will continue to operate correctly after January 1, 2000. However, customers must test integrated systems to see if components work with Hart Scientific manufactured products. Hart makes no representation or warranty concerning non-Hart manufactured products.

And …

> If you're using our equipment with someone else's gear, who the hell knows what's going to happen. We sure don't, so how can we promise you something specific, or even vague for that matter? We can't, so we won't. However, we love our customers and like always we'll do whatever is reasonable to solve whatever problems come up, if there are any.

We seem to know, intuitively, when something spoken, written or recorded is sincere and honest – when it comes from another person's heart, rather than being a synthesis of corporatespeak filtered by myriad iterations of editing, trimming and targeting. There's an inherent pomposity in much of what passes for corporate communication today. Missing are the voice, humour and simple sense of worth and honesty that characterise person-to-person conversation.

We survived Y2K, but that's not the biggest challenge we face. The need for honest speech, to ordinary people, hasn't gone away. Web-savvy consumers are ignoring online brochures. An organisation, as presented via the Web, must have a human voice, must stand for something, mean something, want to meet people, and show they're trying to understand those people.

Millions and millions served

How do you scale one-to-one networking to reach
thousands and millions of like-minded netizens?
Sure, I could do it with a phalanx of smart people
reaching out and touching electronically, but then my
fledgling company's burn rate would increase faster
than I could raise capital. Where is the balance
there? Seems like any mass-produced message
(even tailored for a given 'market') will be
disingenuous to the savvy.

– Jody Lentz, *e-mail to cluetrain.com*

Is having conversations with lots of constituents really practical? Yes. Our conversations are already reaching more customers than we know. People have other means of hearing conversations besides talking to us directly. They can 'eavesdrop' on conversations we have with others by reading other people's e-mail posted to the Web, or by reading posts in newsgroups. The volume of conversation about us that we don't participate in directly is almost always greater than the volume we are personally involved in. We respond not only to the honesty and integrity of our conversations on the Net but also to those indicators of integrity in other people's conversations. Our choice was never to be in all the conversations, but to be honest and open in those we do engage in.

Companies will survive employees telling their truths, their stories in a business context, without instituting draconian controls on their ability to speak out when and to whom they please. We listen to individuals differently than we do to organisational speech. When a company publishes PR, it's trying to give us a complete message about who they are and what they do. We have to decide to trust or distrust the company based on a single statement. Well-written PR leaves us with few avenues for corroboration and second opinions. It's meant to be self-contained.

On the other hand, when I converse with people inside a company, I hear stories from individuals. They're all grains of sand, their combined voices richer and more diverse than the univocal speech of corporate mouthpieces. We add up all the anecdotes we hear from individuals. We have to trust our own averaging, our own summing of stories, our own divining of truth. With more people, more stories in the mix, it's harder for one negative story to sway me. This speaks to the need to have many people in an organisation talking to customers. A single 'corporate story' is a fiction in a world of free conversation. Corporate stories, like corporate cultures, are informed by individuals over time through many contacts, conversations and opportunities to tell stories.

Stories play a large part in the success of organisations. With stories, we teach, pass along knowledge of our craft to colleagues, and create a sense of shared mission. Will co-ordinating what a large number of people have to say be a problem? Yes and no. The problem is not in the effort required to co-ordinate voices, but in the attitude that assumes speech demands co-ordination and control. A culture of story-telling, one encouraging the collection and sharing of knowledge in conversation, may need encouragement and example-setting, but it will certainly fail in the face of attempted restraint.

When we were building Sun's first Intel-based workstation, the 386i, we used mock magazine reviews of the product as a way to test ideas for the design of the computer and the software. As the design progressed, we settled on one 'review' as an example of a magazine article that might appear when the product shipped. The ersatz review was a hit

There is no longer a single source for 'The Truth'. You can no longer download the corporate PR campaign as reality and go from there. You are now hearing many voices, many 'truths', and will have to pick and choose and integrate. A company's fear is that a lone voice with an axe to grind will make up a 'truth' as plausible as anything the Marketing department has come up with, but harmful to the company, and it'll be adopted as the 'truth' irrespective of the facts.

The reality is that when malicious propaganda happens (and it will happen), the truth will out. That is the glorious thing about the markets of opinion; no opinion stands unchallenged. This is the real fear many corporations have of the markets of opinion, that their white propaganda – they are the Galahads of the industry, pure and good and perfect – will also not survive the challenges of the market of opinions.

They're right, they won't. Cope. The corporations will be revealed to be made up of fallible human beings.

Just like us.

– Brian Hurt, *e-mail to cluetrain.com*

with team members: it became a decision yardstick for months of subsequent design and implementation questions. People also started giving copies of the review to customers and using it as a conversation starter with friends and colleagues in other companies. The review wasn't a product pitch – it required a person to deliver it, explain it, and fill in lots of details. It wasn't a data sheet, but a foil for stories and conversations. Its value was not in creating some kind of official spin, but in enabling the reliable transfer of knowledge and new ideas.

There's legal risk in freer communication between employees and customers. Companies accustomed to issuing pronouncements from a single, tightly controlled department find this conversational shift somewhat terrifying. The intersection of the webbed world with business-as-usual leaves much legal ground uncharted. While we're waiting to see how our laws will evolve to meet these realities, it might be prudent for companies to consider which is more damaging: silence, or talking to customers in many individual voices. Is the legal risk posed by unfettered speech always a valid excuse for not speaking?

A critical aspect of success with large numbers of customers lies in listening to them. It's not enough for employees to talk to customers. There must be a way for the fruits of employee conversations to trickle back into an organisation's plans. When Sun started to address the problem of providing technical support to the Java developer community, we made a glaring error. We assumed our answers to technical questions were more valuable than answers from sources outside our group, than answers from our customers.

Sun's first launch of the Java Developer Connection Web site was an unabashed effort to package a fairly sleazy business proposition: selling per-incident support for a poorly supported and less than adequately documented software product. We were doing a lousy job of helping Java developers. A bright marketing wag had the idea to sell people answers to their questions for 100 bucks a pop. When a licensing engineer who dealt with customers day in and day out posed the question, 'Why should they feel good about paying us for answers that should be in the docs, or for consulting on problems caused by the instability of our products?', the marketing people decided to use a bit of sugarcoating. For $495 a year, a customer could purchase a 'subscription' including five questions, called 'support incidents', and a package including technical newsletters and other goodies. Unfortunately, the marketing team focused on providing the hundred-dollar support answers and didn't spend much time setting up the information-publishing pipeline for the sugarcoating. We had fewer than 200 paying customers for the service. Almost all used up their magic answers in less than a month, then started clamouring for the 'real' value, the (grossly understaffed) information subscription that was to be their pipeline to successful use of Java. To add insult to injury, our own cross-divisional inefficiencies cost us $110 for each question answered. You do the maths.

Time for phase two. We shut down the site and relaunched a free service with a few critical new features. The staffing problem hadn't got any better, so we brainstormed ideas for getting the Java community to help us solve their problems. We now have a free site with question-and-answer forums where developers answer each other directly. We added a tap into Sun's Java software bug database and provided a means for developers to add their own notes and work-arounds to our bug information, as well as vote for the bugs they wanted us to fix soonest. A reverse pipeline into the company sent the bug votes to our engineers to help with prioritisation. The site hit 1 million registered members in 2 years, a far cry from the 200 in 6 months that the initial, traditional support efforts yielded. Moreover, the site became a nexus for conversations about our

Here's a definition of that pesky and borderline elitist phrase, *knowledge worker*: A knowledge worker is someone whose job entails having really interesting conversations at work.

The characteristics of conversations map to the conditions for genuine knowledge generation and sharing: they're unpredictable interactions among people speaking in their own voice about something they're interested in. The conversants implicitly acknowledge they don't have all the answers (or else the conversation is really a lecture) and risk being wrong in front of someone else. And conversations overcome the class structure of business, suspending the organisation chart, at least for a little while.

If Knowledge Management aims at making organisations smarter, and that in turn means increasing the quality of conversations, can we please avoid the temptation to create something called Conversation Management?
– David Weinberger

products and services, and for conversations about other people's solutions to our problems.

Symantec took a similarly creative approach when they first launched their Café product, a suite of programming tools for Java developers. They had one person virtually living in the public support newsgroups. He responded to questions, fielded tech support requests, and generally got himself known as a very straight shooter about Symantec's products. He was only one person, but he was almost single-handedly responsible for the developer community's positive take on Symantec. He wasn't there to promote, but strictly to assist. He gave honest answers to hard questions, acknowledged product shortcomings and painted an honest, open picture of the product's strengths and weaknesses. The developer community's collective opinion of Symantec soared.

Another anecdote from the public relations history of Sun's Java team paints an anti-example. In the first year and a half that Sun's Java group existed, members of the engineering team spoke directly with customers and the press. Java grew from a glimmer, a possibility, to a platform with thousands of curious, turned-on early adopters. There was a general perception that Sun's Java team listened, answered questions and was actively engaged with the community of Java developers.

After about eighteen months, the workload grew to such a point that we started shutting down our channels to the outside world. PR and marketing took over much of our contact with the outside world, and we put our heads down to deal with the increasing demands on the engineering team. The reaction from our developers was stated in these precise words many times over: 'you disappeared'. As we went underground, the perception of the Java group in the marketplace changed from 'a small team of great engineers producing neat stuff' to 'a hype engine to push Sun's stock'. In projects that allowed engineers time to come back online more often, customers cut the engineers far more slack in their attempts to get things right than did the customers of their more close-mouthed brethren.

In such scenarios, of course, engaging in trivial conversations can chew up valuable time – though it's a tough call to know what's truly trivial and what deepens credibility in the conversational space. Sometimes responding to a joke with a one-line e-mail laugh can do wonders. We still need to answer all the mail, but we can do things to eliminate some of the more repetitive communication. Generally, people inclined to find answers themselves will seek out a live person when they want one, based on their own needs and ideas. Most of us would rather not be forced into a conversation by inadequate access to key product information. Investment in learning from the one-on-one conversations we have, and adding to the public knowledge base founded on that learning, pay off in freeing up time to have more interesting conversations. I've seen reductions of up to 75 per cent in support e-mail traffic simply by creating informative lists of frequently asked questions (FAQs) and making people aware of them at the point where they're likely to be scratching their heads over a particular type of question. Making certain, of course, the new content isn't written in corporatespeak!

> There are two kinds of FAQs, I realised recently: 1) those that frame questions the company wants you to ask (Q: So how good ARE your products anyway? A: Very very VERY good!!!), and 2) those that acknowledge actual problems and provide solutions. The (1) variety is bullshit PR, while (2) is truly useful.
>
> – Christopher Locke

I try to spread the burden of dealing with customer conversations throughout an organisation. I make everyone spend some time answering questions from customers. Not only do I mine everyone's budget for the support costs (let's face it, by the time I'm trying to find money to answer the mail, it's too late) but I also give everyone involved a tap into our customers' heads. It results in a lot more shared awareness of our mission, strengths and opportunities.

Silence is fatal

Online markets will talk about companies whether companies like it or not. People will say whatever they like, without caring whether they're overheard or quoted – in fact, having one's views passed along is usually the whole point. Companies can't stop customers from speaking up, and can't stop employees from talking to customers. Their only choice is to start encouraging employees to talk to customers – and *empowering* them to act on what they hear. Freed from restrictions perceived as an unwelcome straitjacket, and ultimately unenforceable anyway, workers can generate enormous goodwill as everyday evangelists for products and services they've crafted themselves, and thus take genuine pride in them.

> I've spent the last two years 'bringing fire to the cavemen' in the corporate world (specifically fashion). They still don't understand the difference between a server, a browser, and content, but they do understand that they have to be online. They think that a computer is just like a television. That you can just scan some glossy print ads and throw them up on a site. No one cares about usability. No one cares about being real.
>
> They're scared that if they don't make the jump to Internet marketing/selling that they'll lose their customer loyalty. They're scared that if they do make the jump to Internet marketing/selling that they'll lose their customer loyalty. They ask themselves: 'Is this really us? Is technology part of our lifestyle/branding concept?' They say they don't market to that demographic, but they know deep down inside that if they don't soon they won't have anyone to market to.
>
> Sometimes I just want to scream.
>
> – Kimberly Peterson, *e-mail to cluetrain.com*

'Customer loyalty' is not a commodity a company owns. Where it exists at all – and the cases in which it does are rare – loyalty to a company is based on respect. And that respect is based on how the company has conducted itself in conversations with the market. Not conversing, participating, is not an option. If we don't engage people inside and outside our organisation in conversation, someone else will. Start talking.

Markets are conversations

DOC SEARLS
and David Weinberger

When you think of the Internet,
don't think of Mack trucks full of widgets destined
for distributorships, whizzing by countless billboards.

Think of a table for two.

@man

IT WAS APRIL IN PARIS, several weeks before a big press conference where my client, a large but rapidly shrinking French computer company, would roll out a wonderful new computer, the first of its kind. The whole project had been veiled in secrecy for years. Security was intense. Code names were used. Deep alliances with Big Players were mentioned only in hushed tones. The company had hired me to develop a strategy for the rollout. In particular, they wanted a 'message', one that would serve as a tag line for the event and for all the advertising to follow. A meeting of the company's marketing communications people was convened for my analysis of the market and a briefing on a strategy that would make the press conference great.

The assignment was painfully hopeless. Oh, the new computer was nice and the usual customers would buy it, but the larger market – the one this company needed to penetrate – could care less. The company had been too silent too long. With nothing to lose, I told them the truth.

'We have three problems,' I began. 'First, there is no market for your message, least of all among journalists, who want facts and stories. Second, there is no market for your secrecy. You have long ignored the market, now they will choose to ignore you. Third, there really is no market for your press conference. Journalists want to be briefed exclusively.'

They stared at me. I continued:

'Markets are nothing more than conversations. See these magazines? They're a form of market conversation. We should already be in their stories. We are key to the subject, but we're missing in action after working in secret for years. Our only hope is to talk. Starting now.'

I outlined a strategy for igniting as much conversation as possible in a very short time, suggesting some fun, creative and, ultimately, pointless ideas. Later, a dozen people came up and thanked me for telling the truth and giving them new hope (although presumably for their next jobs).

Then the project manager took me aside and said, 'That was brilliant. Now, what's the tag line?'

First things last

The first markets were markets. Not bulls, bears or invisible hands. Not battlefields, targets or arenas. Not demographics, eyeballs or seats. Most of all, not consumers.

The first markets were filled with people, not abstractions or statistical aggregates; they were the places where supply met demand with a firm handshake. Buyers and sellers looked each other in the eye, met and connected. The first markets were places for exchange, where people came to buy what others had to sell – and to talk.

The first markets were filled with talk. Some of it was about goods and products. Some of it was news, opinion and gossip. Little of it mattered to everyone; all of it engaged someone. There were often conversations about the work of hands: 'Feel this knife. See how it fits your palm.' 'The cotton in this shirt, where did it come from?' 'Taste this apple. We won't have them next week. If you like it you should take some today.' Some of these conversations ended in a sale, but don't let that fool you. The sale was merely the exclamation mark at the end of the sentence.

Market leaders were men and women whose hands were worn by the work they did. Their work was their life, and their brands were the names they were known by: Miller, Weaver, Hunter, Skinner, Farmer, Brewer, Fisher, Shoemaker, Smith.

For thousands of years, we knew exactly what markets were: conversations between people who sought out others who shared the same interests. Buyers had as much to say as sellers. They spoke directly to each other without the filter of media, the artifice of positioning statements, the arrogance of advertising or the shading of public relations.

These were the kinds of conversations people have been having since they started to talk. Social. Based on intersecting interests. Open to many resolutions. Essentially unpredictable. Spoken from the centre of the self. 'Markets were conversations' doesn't mean 'markets were noisy'. It means markets were places where people met to see and talk about each other's work.

Conversation is a profound act of humanity. So once were markets.

The industrial interruption

The advent of the Industrial Age did more than just enable industry to produce products much more efficiently. Management's approach to production and its workers was quickly echoed in its approach to the market and its customers. The economies of scale they were gaining in the factory demanded economies of scale in the market. By the time it was over we had forgotten the one true meaning of the market and replaced it with industrial substitutes.

In third wave, Alvin Toffler wrote that the rise of industry drove an 'invisible wedge' between production and consumption, a fact Friedrich Engels had noticed over 100 years earlier. As production was ramped up to unheard-of rates, the clay pot of craftwork was broken into shards of repetitive tasks that maximised efficiency by minimising difference: interchangeable workers creating interchangeable products.

In the market, consumption also needed to be ramped up – not just to absorb the increased production of goods, but also to promote people's willingness to buy the one-size-fits-all products that rolled off mass-production lines. And management wasted little time noticing the parallels in efficiencies they could achieve all along the production-consumption chain. If products and workers were interchangeable, then interchangeable consumers began to look pretty good too.

The goal was simple. Customers had to be convinced to desire the same thing, the same Model-T in any colour, so long as it's black. And if workers could be better organised through the repetitive nature of their tasks, so customers were more easily defined by the collective nature of their tastes. Just as management developed a new organisational model to enhance economies of scale in production, it developed the techniques of mass marketing to do the same for consumption.

So the customers who once looked you in the eye while hefting your wares in the market were transformed into consumers. In the words of industry analyst Jerry Michalski, a consumer was no more than 'a gullet whose only purpose in life is to gulp products and crap cash'. Power swung so decisively to the supply side that 'market' became a verb: something you do *to* customers.

In the 20th century, the rise of mass communications media enhanced industry's ability to address even larger markets with no loss of shoe leather, and mass marketing truly came into its own. With larger markets came larger rewards, and larger rewards had to be protected. More bureaucracy, more hierarchy and more command and control meant the customer who looked you in the eye was promptly escorted out of the building by security.

The product of mass marketing was the *message*, delivered in as many forms as there were media and in as many guises as there were marketers to invent them.

Delivered locally, shipped globally, repeated inescapably, the business of marketing devoted itself to delivering the message. Unfortunately, the customer never wanted to take delivery.

The shipping view

During the Industrial Age, the movement of materials from production to consumption – from flax to linen and from ore to musket – was a long and complicated process. Potentially vast markets had potentially vast distribution needs. The development of new transportation systems eased the burden, and global systems flourished. Even huge distances could be spanned so that products could be delivered efficiently. Inexorably, business began to understand itself through a peculiar new metaphor: *Business is shipping*. In this shipping metaphor – still the heart and soul of business-as-usual – producers package *content* and move it through a *channel, addressed* for delivery down a *distribution system*.

The metaphor was effectively applied not just to the movement of physical goods, but also quickly applied to the packaging and delivery of marketing content. It's no surprise that business came to think of marketing as simply the delivery of a different type of content to consumers. It was efficient to manage, one size could fit many, and the distribution channel – the new world of broadcast media – was more than ready to deliver. The symmetry was perfect. The production side of business ships interchangeable products and the marketing side ships interchangeable messages, both to the same market, the bigger and more homogeneous, the better.

One problem: *there is no demand for messages*. The customer doesn't want to hear from business, thank you very much. The message that gets broadcast to you, me and the rest of the earth's population has nothing to do with me in particular. It's worse than noise. It's an interruption. It's the Anti-Conversation.

That's the awful truth about marketing. It broadcasts messages to people who don't want to listen. Every advertisement, press release, publicity stunt and giveaway engineered by a Marketing department is coloured by the fact that it's going to a public that doesn't ask to hear it.

Marketers felt this truth in their bones and learned to cloak their messages, to disguise them as entertainment, to repackage the content as regularly as business learned to vary this year's product line. Today, we all know and have come to expect this. We are even disappointed if it's not well done. Commercials disguise themselves as one-act plays, press releases play the part of important stories, and advertising masquerades as education. Marketing became an elaborate game between business and the consumer, but the outcome remained fixed. As sophisticated as marketing became, it has never overcome the ability of people to smell the BS behind all the marketing perfume.

It is not hard to understand, then, that 'business is shipping' at times felt more like 'business is war', another pervasive metaphor. We *launch* marketing campaigns based on *strategies* that *target* markets; we *bombard* people with messages in order to *penetrate* markets (and the sexual overtones here shouldn't be dismissed either). Business-as-usual is in a constant state of war with the market, with the Marketing department manning the front lines.

Consider the distance we've come. Markets once were places where producers and customers met face-to-face and engaged in conversations based on shared interests. Now business-as-usual is engaged in a grinding war of attrition with its markets.

No wonder marketing fails.

The axe in our heads

Every one of us knows that marketers are out to get us, and we all struggle to escape their snares. We channel-surf through commercials; we open our mail over the recycling bin, struggling to discern the junk mail without having to open the envelope; we resent the adhesion of commercial messages to everything from sports uniforms to escalator risers.

We know that the real purpose of marketing is to insinuate the message into our consciousness, to put an axe in our heads without our noticing. Like it or not, they will teach us to sing the jingle and recite the slogan. If the axe finds its mark we toe the line, buy the message, buy the product and don't talk back. For the axe of marketing is also meant to silence us, to make conversation in the market as unnecessary as the ox cart.

Ironically, many of us spend our days wielding axes ourselves. In our private lives we defend ourselves from the marketing messages out to get us, our defences made stronger for having spent the day at work trying to drive axes into our customers' heads. We do both because the axe is already there, the metaphorical embodiment of that wedge Toffler wrote about – the one that divides our jobs from our lives. On the supply side is the producer; on the demand side is the consumer. In the caste system of industry, it is bad form for the two to exchange more than pleasantries.

Thus the system is quietly maintained, and our silence goes unnoticed beneath the noise of marketing-as-usual. No exchange between seller and buyer, no banter, no conversation. And hold the handshakes.

When you have the combined weight of 200 years of history and a trillion-dollar tide of marketing pressing down on the axe in your head, you can bet it's wedged in there pretty good. What's remarkable is that now there's a force potent enough to actually start loosening it.

> **As seen on TV**
>
> It isn't just working consumers who suffer from axe-in-head disease. CEOs have the same problem. Even hip e-CEOs like Bob Davis of Lycos, Inc. 'We're a media company,' Davis tells PC Week. 'We make our money by delivering an audience that people want to pay for.' Note the two different species here: *audience* and *people*. And look at their qualities. One is 'delivered'. The other pays. One is cargo and the other is money. Never mind that we're talking about the *Web* here. Customers – and advertisers – are human. Consumers are not.

Here's the voice of a spokesperson from the world of TV itself, Howard Beale, the anchorman in Paddy Chayefsky's NETWORK who announced that he would commit suicide because 'I just ran out of bullshit'. Of course, he had to go insane before he could at last utter this truth and pull the axe from his own head.

Networked markets

The long silence – the industrial interruption of the human conversation – is coming to an end. On the Internet, markets are getting more connected and more powerfully vocal every day. These markets want to talk, just as they did for the thousands of years that passed before *market* became a verb with *us* as its object.

The Internet is a *place*. We buy books and tickets *on* the Web. Not *over*, *through* or *beside* it. To call it a 'platform' belies its hospitality. What happens on the Net is more than commerce, more than content, more than push and pull and clicks and traffic and *e*-anything. The Net is a *real place* where people can go to learn, to talk to each other and to do business together. It is a bazaar where customers look for wares, vendors spread goods for display and people gather around topics that interest them. It is a conversation. At last and again.

In this new place, every product you can name, from fashion to office supplies, can be discussed, argued over, researched and bought as part of a vast conversation among the people interested in it. 'I'm in the market for a new computer,' someone says, and she's off to the Dell site. But she probably won't buy that cool new laptop right away. She'll ask around first – on Web pages, on newsgroups, via e-mail: 'What do you think? Is this a good one? Has anybody checked it out? What's the real battery life? How's their customer support? Recommendations? Horror stories?'

'I'm in the market for a good desk dictionary,' says someone else, and he's off to Amazon.com where he'll find a large number of opinions already expressed:

> I love the look of this book, and the publisher did a great job; but I made the mistake of buying it without realizing that it was first published over 7 years ago …

> I've had this book for two days and I keep going back to it. I may not be typical since I collect dictionaries and wanted this when I heard about it last year, but …

> Ugh, they don't have 'aegritudo' but they have the 'modern' definition of 'peruse' …

These conversations are most often about value: the value of products and of the businesses that sell them. Not just prices, but the market currencies of reputation, location, position and every other quality that is subject to rising or falling opinion.

It's nothing new, in one sense. The only advertising that was ever truly effective was word of mouth, which is nothing more than conversation. Now word of mouth has gone global. The one-to-many scope that technology brought to mass production and then mass marketing, which producers have enjoyed for 200 years, is now available to customers. And they're eager to make up for lost time.

More ominous for marketing-as-usual is this: finding themselves connected to one another in the market doesn't enable customers just to learn the truth behind product claims. The very sound of the Web conversation throws into stark relief the monotonous, lifeless, self-centered drone emanating from Marketing departments around the world. Word of Web offers people the pure sound of the human voice, not the elevated, empty speech of the corporate hierarchy. Further, these voices are telling one another the truth based on their real experiences, unlike the corporate messages that aim at presenting what we can generously call a best-case scenario. Not only can the market discover the truth in the time it takes to do a search at a discussion archive, but the tinny, self-absorbed voices of business-as-usual sound especially empty in contrast to the rich conversations emanating from the Web.

What's more, networked markets get smart fast. Metcalfe's Law,* a famous axiom of the computer industry, states that the value of a network increases as the square of the number of users connected to it – connections multiply value exponentially. This is also true for conversations on networked markets. In fact, as the network gets larger it also gets *smarter*. *The Cluetrain Corollary*: the level of knowledge on a network increases as the square of the number of users times the volume of conversation. So, in market conversations, it is far easier to learn the truth about the products being pumped, about the promises being made, and about the people making those promises. Networked markets are not only smart markets, but they're also equipped to get much smarter, much faster, than business-as-usual.

....

* Bob Metcalfe is the inventor of Ethernet, the founder of 3Com, and an INFOWORLD columnist, among many other vocations.

Business-as-usual doesn't realise this because it continues to conceptualise markets as distant abstractions – battlefields, targets, demographics – and the Net as simply another conduit down which companies can broadcast messages. But the Net isn't a conduit, a pipeline or another television channel. The Net invites your customers in to talk, to laugh with each other, and to learn from each other. Connected, they reclaim their voice in the market, but this time with more reach and wider influence than ever.

When push comes to suck

The reluctance of business-as-usual to break out of its set way of thinking was perhaps epitomised best by the Web's own infatuation with 'push technology'. This reached its zenith in May 1997, when Wired, the computer industry's utopian fashion monthly, boldly declared its wish to supplant the Web with media more suited to advertising. In its customary overstatement and retinal-torture colours, the magazine devoted its cover and following 11 pages to 'PUSH! Kiss your browser Goodbye: The radical future of media beyond the Web.' According to the article, the Web was already too demanding for the average spud, so *Wired* wanted your inner couch potato to enjoy 'a more full-bodied experience that combines many of the traits of networks with those of broadcast. *Seinfeld* viewers know what we're talking about,' the authors wrote.

Ever since the Web showed up, business-as-usual has desperately tried to pipe-weld it onto the back end of TV's history. The money at stake is huge. McCann-Erickson reports more than $45.5 billion spent on TV advertising in the United States alone in 1998. In the same year, total worldwide advertising expenses passed $400 billion. That'll keep a lot of axes in a lot of heads.

But it won't work on the Web, because networked markets aren't passive spectators waiting to receive the next marketing message. The Web isn't home to advertising-as-usual. The 'push' movement of 1997 became the pushover of 1998.

The market that talk built

The power of conversation goes well beyond its ability to affect consumers, business and products. Market conversations can make – and unmake and remake – entire industries. We're seeing it happen now. In fact, the Internet itself is an example of an industry built by pure conversation.

The process of building the Internet was a little like building a bridge: start with a thin wire spanning a chasm, then spin that single wire into a thick cable capable of supporting heavy girders and the rest of the structure. Incredibly, no one directed this effort. No one controlled it. The people who incrementally built the Internet – literally, one bit at a time – participated solely out of enthusiasm, an enthusiasm driven by a shared and growing vision of what this strange thing they were building might ultimately become.

What if the task of building the Internet had been jobbed out to the leaders of the communications business: to online services like AOL and Compuserve, to network companies like Novell and 3Com, to telecom companies like AT&T and Northern Telecom, to software companies like Microsoft and Lotus?

It never would have happened. It certainly never would have been imagined as it now exists. Every one of those companies would have looked for a way to control it, to make it theirs. More than a few would have turned down the job. Microsoft was famously late to the Internet game in part because Bill Gates thought there was no money to be made.

What it took was behind-the-scenes work by what amounts to a loosely organised, Internet-mediated software craft guild. The results include Apache, a Web server developed by Brian Behlendorf and a bunch of other hackers, simply because they needed it. Today more than half of all the Web's pages are served by Apache.

In fact, nearly a third of the world's Web servers are powered by Linux, the dark-horse challenger to Microsoft's previously unquestioned software hegemony. Linux was initiated by a young, unknown software developer, Linus Torvalds. He needed it, so he crafted it – and then he made it available to the rest of the world through the Internet. He published not just the finished product but, far more important, its source code. Anyone with software engineering tools and the technical chops could add to it, modify it, craft it into precisely the tool they needed. As a result, Linux has rapidly become one of the most sophisticated, powerful and configurable software products in history – all without anyone managing or controlling it.

Eric Raymond, in his seminal work on hacker culture, *The Cathedral and the Bazaar*, describes the dynamics of this distributed and self-motivated community of independent programmers. How was it possible that a seemingly disorganised, seemingly undirected band of renegade hackers could rise to such prominence and threaten the world's largest, most powerful high-tech corporation with the only credible alternative not only to Windows NT, but even to Windows itself?

By conversation. Both the Internet and Linux are powerful demonstrations of a pure market conversation at work. They show what can happen when people are able to communicate without either the constraints of command-and-control management or the straightjacket of one-message-fits-all. As Raymond writes:

> The thing about the Internet is you can't coerce people over a T-1 line, so power relationships don't work ... So the only game left to play is pure craftsmanship and reputation among peers. If you can offer people the chance to do good work and be seen doing good work by their peers, that's a really powerful motivator.

The most important lesson Linux hackers teach is that *whole markets* can rapidly arise out of conversations that are independent not only of business, but also of government, education and other powerful but hidebound institutions, thanks in large measure to something hackers helped invent precisely for that purpose: the Internet.

Conversation may be a distraction in factories that produce replaceable products for replaceable consumers, but it's intimately tied to the world of craft, where the work of hands expresses the voice of the maker. Conversation is how the work of craft groups proceeds. And conversation is the sound of the market where creators and customers are close enough to feel each other's heat.

What's more, these new conversations needn't just happen at random. They can be created on purpose. 'We hackers were actively *aiming* to create new kinds of conversations outside of traditional institutions,' Raymond says. 'This wasn't an accidental byproduct of doing neat techie stuff; it was an explicit goal for many of us as far back as the 1970s. We *intended* this revolution.'

Nice job.

New messages for marketing

So, if markets are conversations (they are) and there's no market for messages (there isn't), what's marketing-as-usual to do? *Own* the conversations? Keep the conversations *on message*? Turn up the volume until it drowns out the market? *Compete* with the new conversations?

But how could it? People are talking in the new market because they want to, because they're interested, because it's fun. Conversations are the 'products' the new markets are 'marketing' to one another constantly online. Hey! Come look at my Web site. Subscribe to my e-zine. Check the whacked-out rant I just posted to **alt.transylvanian.polarbears**. Get a load of this stupid banner ad I just found at **boy-are-we-clueless.com**!

By comparison, corporate messaging is pathetic. It's not funny. It's not interesting. It doesn't know who we are, or care. It only wants us to buy. If we wanted more of that, we'd turn on the TV. But we don't and we won't. We're too busy. We're too wrapped up in some fascinating conversation.

Engagement in these open free-wheeling marketplace exchanges isn't optional. It's a prerequisite to *having* a future. Silence is fatal.

So what becomes of marketing? How do companies enter into the global conversation? How do they find their own voice? Can they? How do they wean themselves from messaging? What happens to:

- PR
- advertising
- marketing communications
- pricing
- positioning

… and the rest of the marketing arsenal?

Excellent questions.

Private relations

Ironically, public relations has a huge PR problem: people use it as a synonym for BS. The call of the flack has never been an especially honourable one. There is no Pulitzer Prize for public relations. No Peabody, Heismann, Oscar, Emmy, Eddy or Flacky. Like all besieged professions, PR has its official bodies, which do indeed grant various awards, degrees and titles. But do you know what they are? Neither do most PR people. Say that you're an award-winning PR person and most people will want to change their seats.

Everyone – including many PR people – senses that something is deeply phony about the profession. And it's not hard to see what it is. Take the standard computer-industry press release. With few exceptions, it describes an 'announcement' that was not made, for a product that was not available, quoting people who never said anything, for distribution to a list of people who mostly consider it trash.

Dishonesty in PR is *pro forma*. A press release is written as a plainly fake news story, with headline, dateline, quotes and all the dramatic tension of a phone number. The idea, of course, is to make the story easy for editors to 'insert' in their publications.

But an editor would rather insert a crab in his butt than a press release in his publication. The disconnection between supply and demand could hardly be more extreme. No self-respecting editor would let a source – least of all a biased one – write a story. And no editor is in the market for a thinly disguised advertisement, which is the actual content of a press release.

Editors hate having to deconstruct press releases to find just the facts, ma'am. To most editors, press releases are just pretend clothing for emperors best seen naked – because naked emperors make much better stories than dressed-up ones.

PR folk are paid to hate stories, even though stories are precisely what the press – PR's 'consumers' – most wants. The fundamental appeal of stories is conflict, struggle and complexity. Stories never begin with 'happily ever after', but press releases always do, because that's the kind of story PR's real market – the companies who pay for public relations – demands. The PR version of the Titanic story would be headlined **705 Delighted Passengers Arrive after the *Titanic*'s Maiden Voyage**. Page two might mention some 'shakedown glitches inevitable whenever a magnificent new ship is launched'. Releases have no room for the very elements that might actually interest a journalist.

Public relations not only fails to comprehend the nature of stories, but imagines that 'positive' stories can be 'created' with press conferences and other staged events. John C. Dvorak, PR scourge of long standing, says, 'So why would you want to sit in a large room full of reporters and publicly ask a question that can then be quoted by every guy in the place? It's not the kind of material a columnist wants – something everybody is reporting. I'm always amazed when PR types are disappointed when I tell them I won't be attending a press conference.'

The real role of press releases

Press releases serve some functions other than pretending to attempt to get ink:

- They let a company try on and then decide on a positioning: 'Here's how our story would appear in the press.'

- They tell your boss that you're doing an excellent job: 'We shipped the Rangolator 2000 on time, and it's the first uniquely revolutionary enterprise Web-based portal solutioniser. See, it says so right in this fake newspaper article, boss!'

- They give management the illusion that they're going to be quoted in a magazine article.

It'd be nice if companies figured out that they can do all that without actually wasting editors' time with the damn press releases.

'PR types.' We all know what that means: they're the used car salesmen of the corporate world. You can't listen to PR Types without putting on your highest-grade, activated-carbon bullshit filter. If you're a journalist, you are seen by PR Types as prey. They hunt you down at work, at social events – hell, if you're donating a kidney and a PR Type is on the next table, she'll chat you up about the new product announcement until her anaesthetic kicks in and then a little bit longer. Damn PR Types.

But, of course, the best of the people in PR are not PR Types at all. They understand that they aren't censors, they're the company's best conversationalists. Their job – their *craft* – is to discern stories the market actually wants to hear, to help journalists write stories that tell the truth, to bring people into conversation rather than protect them from it. Indeed, already some companies are building sites that give journalists comprehensive, unfiltered information about the industry, including unedited material from their competitors. In the age of the Web where hype blows up in your face and spin gets taken as an insult, the real work of PR will be more important than ever.

Advertising vs word of Web

Fairfax Cone, one of the great men of advertising, said his craft was nothing more than 'what you do when you can't go see somebody'. This simple distinction draws a perfect line between TV and the Web. TV is the best medium ever created for advertising. The Web is the best medium ever created for sales. The Web, like the telephone, is a way you can go and see somebody, a way to talk with them, show your wares, answer their questions, offer referrals, and make it easy for them to buy whatever they want. Why get someone to look at an ad on the Web when, with exactly the same amount of wrist power, you can get them into your electronic storefront itself?

Sure, you can advertise on the Web, and many Internet companies say advertising is how they are going to make their money. And the sum of advertising on the Web keeps going up. Why not? Just liquidate a few per cent of those moon-high stock valuations and buy a few billion dollars more Web advertising. Forrester Research reports that 'despite cries that online ads don't work, spending for Internet advertising will continue to grow at a furious pace'. They say spending will explode from $2.8 billion in 1999 to $33 billion in 2004.

But Web advertising is already an inside joke. Most of the banner ads you see at the tops of pages are trades and sponsorships, not paid advertising. And everybody knows that having your page turn up in the top ten results when someone goes hunting at a major search site is far more effective than buying ads on Web sites. (This, predictably, has sparked the buying of ads on *search* sites.)

There's no denying that a saturation ad campaign that puts your company's name in tens of millions of banner ads will buy you some name recognition. But that recognition counts for little against the tidal wave of word-of-Web. Look at how this already works in today's Web conversation. You want to buy a new camera. You go to the sites of the three camera makers you're considering. You hastily click through the brochureware the vendors paid thousands to have designed, and you finally find a page that actually gives straightforward factual information. Now you go to a Usenet discussion group, or you find an e-mail list on the topic. You read what real customers have to say. You see what questions are being asked and you're impressed with how well other buyers – strangers from around the world – have answered them. You learn that the model you're interested in doesn't really work as well in low light as the manufacturer's page says. You make a decision. A year later, some stranger in a discussion group asks how reliable the model you bought is. You answer. You tell the truth.

Compare that to the feeble sputtering of an ad. 'SuperDooper Glue – Holds Anything!' says your ad. 'Unless you flick it sideways – as I found out with the handle of my favourite cup,' says a little voice in the market. 'BigDisk Hard Drives – Lifetime Guarantee!' says the ad. 'As long as you can prove you oiled it three times a week,' says another little voice in the market. What these little voices used to say to a single friend is now accessible to the world. No number of ads will undo the words of the market. How long does it take until the market conversation punctures the exaggerations made in an ad? An hour? A day? The speed of word of mouth is now limited only by how fast people can type. Word of Web will trump word of hype, every time.

Ads may still have hypnotic, subliminal effects, like those tunes we can't get out of our heads (a legacy of the old advertising industry adage 'if you have nothing to say, sing it'), but we now have the world's largest support group encouraging us to take that first step: we acknowledge that there is a power greater than ourselves, and it's not some freaking banner ad or a cola company whacking our head with a jingle. It's the conversation that is the Web.

Sites of salt

You might think Marketing Communications departments talk about communications. Not really. They actually spend most of their days thinking about how to hide what's really going on in the organisation. That's what crafting 'messages' is mostly about. For every 'message', there are dozens or hundreds of facts – interesting, useful facts – that never get said. Numbers that change. Divisions that move. Features added and subtracted. And that's not counting all the outright negative stuff: the merger that failed, the layoffs, the departed leaders, the stopgap products.

In the Industrial Age – the age of scarce and mostly nonconversational media – there were legitimate reasons for being 'on message'. The biggest was the need to say one positive thing to everybody at once, in a form that worked equally well in a 30-second ad and a 30-page white paper to reach the broadest common denominator.

Even at their most complete – in the form of brochures and other stiff-necked paper goods – marketing communications painted a glossy picture no one believed. We all have been trained by a lifetime of experience to turn down the volume when confronted with a beautiful full-colour artefact explaining why the products are perfect, the company loves its customers, and every customer is delighted. Like editors skimming a press release, customers root through brochures to find a few motes of useful information. We took all of 'marcom's' goods with more than a pinch of salt. We needed a whole salt mine to keep up with the tide of BS.

Predictably, most corporate Web sites look like brochures. Visitors have to click through screen after screen of fatuous self-praise to find the few bits of useful information they really want. At least printed brochures don't take as long to download.

If you want to take your first baby step towards entering the market conversation, torch any brochureware on your site. At best your networked market views it as a speed bump, at worst as an insult.

Dunk this!

As the Internet shifts the power from merchants to customers you can hear the timbers creaking. For instance, David Felton was mightily – perhaps a tad irrationally – cheesed off when a Dunkin' Donuts shop refused to put skimmed milk into his coffee, even though the sign in the window said you can get it 'your way' there. So he did what any red-blooded Internet denizen would do: he made fun of Dunkin' Donuts on his Web site. And then he grabbed **www.dunkin-donuts.org** and turned it into a public comment board.

The comments poured in – predominantly negative. Some seemed not worth the calories it took to type them: 'I would like to know why the DD on the Fellsway in Medford requires that I buy at least 5 munchkins … If I wanted 5 munchkins I would get a donut.' Others were a bit more biting: 'I live quite close to [a particular store] and only smell donuts being baked about once a week …' And then there's the employee who warned people to stay away from anything filled with jelly since the employees 'toss it around, play with it'.

The 5000 franchise owners jumped into the fray. Said Felton in a press release: 'It was a common occurrence to see a comment about a particular franchise submitted in the morning, and by the same afternoon, the owner of the franchise already contacted the author and submitted a follow-up on the Web site.' But that wasn't enough for the Corporate Big Boys with their big swingin' jelly sticks. They sued the little guy, even though he was getting only 50 to 70 visitors a day. Felton sold the site to Dunkin' for an undisclosed sum. He says he couldn't face the legal bills and harassment. One of the terms is that Dunkin' host a public comment area on its own site. As of this writing, it's not clear that they will post the comments or just suck them into the 'Customer Service department', where they will be processed into a crusty new fudge topping prepared by employees who don't wash their hands.

But, if Dunkin' Donuts lacks the munchkins to let the public speak, the public will find another site to do it: **www.dunkindonutssucks.com** is already registered.

That doesn't mean that you should put up a site that consists of nothing but the facts, expressed in Times Roman text (although useful facts are a great place to start). Your site needs to have a voice, to express a point of view, and to give access to helpful people inside your corporation. Replace the brochures with ways to ignite dialogues. Not only do your customers want to talk with real people inside your organisation, but your employees are desperate to talk with real customers. They want to tell them the truth.

They will in any event, because your wall of brochures is as solid as a line in the sand.

Fair market price

Traditionally, Marketing departments engage in pricing exercises to discover a market's ceiling. This makes obvious sense when the supply side controls the means of both production and distribution. But after the revolution, comrade, the old regime's pricing strategies are the first to be led to the gibbet. After decades of replaceable products, replaceable workers and replaceable consumers, we now have replaceable *merchants*. Think of this as the mass market's revenge.

The first effect of this shift in power has been tremendous downward price pressure. After being trained so assiduously in the economics of mass-ness, the first impulse on the Web is to shop on price alone. Shopping 'bots' can find the lowest price among all merchants doing business on the Web. I can go to **www.InvoiceDealers.com** and see a head-to-head comparison of how little over the invoice price my local car dealers are willing to sell me a new Honda. Or if I decide to buy an Epson Stylus 900 colour printer (I have already listened in on the consumer conversations on the Web), I can go to a site like **www.computeresp.com** and get a list of 44 merchants, sorted by price, that will sell me one for prices ranging from $330.95 to $404.37. Some of the merchant names may be familiar – Egghead ($346.39) and Gateway ($364.95) – but how much is name recognition worth given that whatever service I may need is going to require the same trip to the post office anyway?

Driving margins towards zero isn't a good thing. Businesses have to make money, after all. And in a war of margin slicing, the Big Boys are often able to stand the heat longer (although A&P managed to burn itself to the ground in the 1970s by initiating a competition with smaller grocery stores to see who could price the furthest under cost for the longest). But it's early yet. And merchants are smart. They offer new services that will distract the market from its insistence on extracting vengeance by shaving margins with a guillotine. And what are those emerging services, hmm? *Conversations.*

For example, the merchant may enable you to talk with its own experts. Or it may put you in touch with the rest of the market directly, using the means the Web has served up to us. Amazon.com famously presents readers' reviews and rankings. For technical support, Microsoft directs you to Usenet-style discussion groups, which it's smart enough not to try to control.

In short, although there is no demand for messages, there is a tremendous demand for good conversation. That's one way merchants fight commoditisation. But both no-margin pricing and higher-margin pricing with the added value of conversation are still examples of pricing driven from on high as if suppliers were still in charge. Increasingly, they're not. In fact, in the most exciting new markets developing on the Web, the demand side – the market – tells the suppliers just what they're willing to pay. This is quite literally true at **www.priceline.com**, where you can let hotels, airlines, mortgage companies and car dealerships know exactly what your best offer is. They can take your business or leave it. That's up to them. But the pricing is up to you.

The most dramatic move away from top-down pricing is evident at auction sites such as **www.ebay.com**, which enable the market to sell to itself. Yes, eBay is a virtual flea market, albeit it with millions of items on sale at any one moment. But it is also much more. Soon after eBay took off, some merchants realised that they don't need a Web storefront of their own; they can just offer their wares at the auction site. They lose some control over pricing – in a complete role reversal, the market sets the price and the merchant has the power to say no – but they get into the thick of the fray with almost no startup or marketing costs. And it's not just consumers who are engaged in auctions. PNC Bank Corp. in Pittsburgh accepts bids on interest rates for certificates of deposit. Deere & Co. auctions used farm equipment. Ford Motor has auctioned automotive components.

Now the Web is reaching even further up the chain, fundamentally changing the value and cost equations that rationalise pricing. With the music encoding standard called MP3, any digital recording – such as tracks from a CD – can be posted on a Web site, downloaded, listened to, and even recorded back onto a CD. Everyone who knows how to point and click can gather tracks from their favourite musicians and assemble their own albums. Production and distribution are so cheap and easy that the market can do it for itself. That leaves the recording industry with almost nothing but the role of marketing, a task they generally haven't grasped very well when it comes to the Web because they're too busy trying to squelch what they rightly see as a threat to their hegemony. Recording companies thought they were originators but instead found they were intermediaries. And the most efficient markets tend to have the fewest intermediaries.

Which brings us to the top of the chain: in this case, the musicians themselves.

Why would musicians allow their music to be downloaded for free rather than sold for $15–20 by a recording company? Maybe because it's a good marketing technique for selling CDs and concert tickets. Maybe because they hope that fans will eventually be willing to pay them something – much less than the price of a typical CD – for the download privilege, just as shareware has proved a successful business model for many software developers. Maybe musicians will allow their music to be priced low enough to encourage the widest possible distribution because they are *craftspeople* who care more deeply about the value of their work than its price. And maybe it's because they define that value in terms other than what they charge for one form of finished goods.

Waiting for e-books

It doesn't take a genius to see that what MP3 is doing to the music business, the widespread availability of reading matter on the Web will do to the publishing industry. It's already happening. And it will take off like wildfire the moment truly readable, portable computer displays enter the mainstream.

And that is marketing's final pricing challenge. Pricing interchangeable products for a mass market is just a matter of testing how high you can raise the bait out of the water and still have the fish bite. Set the price, maybe tweak it, and you're done: all the fish are going to have to pay the same price. But when it comes to prices, the Web acts like a craft world in which prices aren't uniform across all the products. Each hotel room, each Beanie Baby, and each hand-assembled CD can now be priced according to different rules, granting the customer new advantages. The mechanical transactions in which the price declared by the supplier was paid by the consumer now becomes more of a dance, sometimes a courtship, and always a conversation.

Assume the position

Every morning when I wake up,
I try to remember who I am and where I come from.

Harry S. Truman

Public relations, advertising, and marcom all reflect the company's 'position'. Positioning is darned important, then. Strategic, even. And if you're a marketing consultant, positioning is where the big bucks are. You're right there at the top of the marketing totem pole.

Positioning is not only lucrative for its practitioners, it's also fun, since it's usually done on a blank piece of paper. 'Who do we want to be?' asks the positioning expert. 'Are we the maker of the world's finest timepieces? No, maybe we're the people who keep business on time. Ooh, maybe we're the company that's making punctuality into a fashion accessory!' Undoubtedly, someone will trump these suggestions by saying, 'We're not really about watches at all,' and then, in a solemn voice: 'We're the Time Company.'

Often, 'positioning exercises' become expensive sojourns into corporate psychology. The consultant gets to spend time with one group leader after another, performing the role of corporate shrink. The resulting data is impossible to connect, but that doesn't matter, because the goal is only to come up with a 'statement'. And all that statement has to be is marginally different from every other company's faked-up statement. Never mind that nobody in the marketplace gives a damn about any company's positioning statement. It only matters that *this* statement will 'drive the strategy', which will be yet another advertising and PR bombing campaign.

Can it get more arrogant? Well, actually, yes.

Positioning wasn't even an issue until 1972, when Al Ries and Jack Trout wrote a series of articles for *Advertising Age* and then authored one of the top-selling business books of all time, *Positioning: The Battle for Your Mind*. The goal of positioning, Trout says, is to own *one word* in your customer's mind. For evidence, you don't even need to leave your own skull. Take a look: you'll find Fedex in the 'overnight' position, Crest in the 'cavities' position, and Volvo in the 'safety' position, even if you never buy those products. In the battlefield of your mind, those companies are entrenched in those positions.

Why one word? Because to Trout and Ries, the human mind is as closed as a clam and just as roomy. Witness Jack Trout's 'five basic principles of the mind,' from *The New Positioning*:

1. Minds are limited.
2. Minds hate confusion.
3. Minds are insecure.
4. Minds don't change.
5. Minds lose focus.

In short, minds are so pathetic that they desperately need help, even if it comes in the form of an axe. That's what positioning is for.

Too bad, because positioning actually is about something much more important, something that gets trivialised by those who reduce it to generating a catchy tag line. Positioning is about discovering who you, as a business, are – *discovering* your identity, not inventing a new one willy-nilly. Positioning should help a company become what it is, not something it's not (no matter how cool it would be).

A company can certainly try to be what it's not. But the market conversation will expose the fakery. One clue is any attempt by a company to deny its history, because history is one of those things that just can't be changed. GM will always be the product of Alfred Sloan's preference for implementation over innovation, Apple will always come from Steve Jobs's artistic temperament, Hewlett-Packard will always come from its founders' obsession with quality products for niche technical markets, Nordstrom will always come from the family's original shoe business.

Of course companies and products can change their identities (and even their natures) over time. Volkswagen no longer bears (for most of us) the history stated in its very name: Hitler's car for the proud German people. Kellogg's Razzle Dazzle Rice Krispies no longer bear much connection to the obsessive health concerns of the company's founder. But such changes generally are gradual and often painful. In fact, if they are too rapid and too easy, the market conversation will be merciless in exposing the phoniness it sniffs.

There are other clues that a company is having an identity crisis:

1. Is there a spark of life in its marketing materials? Do they smack of focus groups and the safety of the lowest common denominator, or do they take the risk of being as interesting as its best customers?

2. Do its marketing programmes keep people out or invite them in? Do they help customers and prospects make connections to the relevant employees?

3. Is the company able to admit a mistake? Can employees admit they disagree with management decisions or the latest marketing mantra? Or must they always explain why everything is perfect in this, the best of all possible companies?

4. Is the company so jealous of its 'image' that it has surgically implanted a lawyer where its sense of humour used to be?

5. Does it drill its employees on the corporate catechism, or can the workers tell stories that for them capture the essence of what the company is about?

6. Do the employees routinely sign their e-mail 'Views expressed do not necessarily reflect those of the management'?

These indicators have a common theme. Each points to a gap between who your company is and what it says it is. The gap is where inauthenticity lives, and the exposure of the gap constitutes corporate embarrassment. Much of marketing is devoted to papering over that gap. Deming gave the deathless advice: 'Drive out fear.' We might add: and drive out shame.

But how can a business be authentic? Authenticity describes whether someone truly owns up to what she or he actually is. Since corporations and businesses aren't individuals, ultimately their authenticity is rooted in the employees. If the company is posing, then the people who *are* the company will have to pose as well. If, on the other hand, the company is comfortable living up to what it is, then an enormous cramp in the corporate body language goes away. The marketing people won't create throwaway lines that are clever but false. The sales folk will walk away from the 'sales opportunities' that the company is better off losing than having to support. The product developers won't propose features that look good on paper but do their customers no real good.

None of this has to do with one-word positioning statements, press release boilerplate or pledging allegiance to corporate goals before every company meeting. It has to be learned in the heart, not by rote. What we learn through memorisation affords us no spontaneity. We can recite the right words, but they're not our own – we can't riff on them. The market conversation can spot marketing recitatives within two syllables because the Web thrives on spontaneity. We are all so tuned to the sound of the real human voice that, given a chance to interact, we can't be fooled … at least not for long.

And if a company is genuinely confused about what it is, there's an easy way to find out: listen to what your market says you are. If it's not to your liking, think long and hard before assuming that the market is wrong, composed of a lot of people who just are too dumb or blind to understand the Inner You. If you've been claiming to be the Time Company for two years but the market still thinks of you as the Overpriced Executive Trophy Watchmaker, then, sorry, but that's your position. If you don't like what you're hearing, the marketing task is not to change the market's *idea* of who you are but *actually* to change who you are. And that can take a generation: look at Volkswagen.

Entering the conversation

The chapters on PR, ads, marcom, pricing, positioning – hell, all of them – in *The Marketing-as-Usual Manual of Strategy and Tactics* need to be redone. It's not because the war has shifted from the air to the ground, or because now we're fighting guerrillas instead of massed troops. No, marketing-as-usual thinks it's fighting a war when in fact the 'enemy' is having a party: 'Hey, dude, put on this Hawaiian shirt, grab some chips and dip, and join in. But first you gotta loosen your grip on that assault weapon.'

Here's some advice on entering the conversation: Loosen up. Lighten up. And shut up for a while. Listen for a change. Marketing-as-usual used to be able to insert its messages into the mind of the masses with one swing of its mighty axe. Now messages get exploded within minutes. 'Spin' gets noticed and scorned. Parodies spread ad campaigns faster than any multimillion-dollar advertising blitz. In short: the Internet routes around a-holes.

So, enter the conversation and do it right. But how?

Corporate voice

Here's a syllogism. Your company needs to engage in the new market conversations. Conversations occur in human voices. Your voice is the public expression of your authentic identity, of who you really are, of where you really come from. So let's draw the logical conclusion: on the Net at least, your company can't engage in the market conversation without its authentic voice.

Sounds simple. But what does it mean when applied to a corporation? Corporations don't have voices. They don't have mouths to speak with, or hands to type with, or body language

Funny

The Web is a funny place – literally. We learn a lot about the voices we hear through their humour. Having a sense of humour tells us that you have some distance from yourself and the dreadful seriousness of your concerns. It is, in most cases, a prerequisite for personal authenticity – if you're not laughing at yourself, are you really being honest about yourself? After all, you are – like all of us – a ridiculous creature.

to betray their real intentions, or eyebrows to punctuate a joke. Corporations are legal fictions.

But *businesses* aren't fictions. Businesses are as real as families and nations. As with all social entities, they speak as the sum of the parts, as the individuals who *are* the parts, and everything in between.

A business has a voice. You can usually hear it – authentic or unauthentic – most obviously and transparently, on its Web site. Even before the last graphic finishes downloading, you can usually tell if the company speaks with passion, if it's lost or uninterested, or if it's online just because some consultant said it has to be. You can tell if the business has some perspective on itself or whether it's all wrapped up in being the Number One Provider of Something, Anything, Please! You can tell if it wants to talk with you or just to pick your pocket. You can tell if the people who work there really care or if they always carry their résumé with them, just in case. You can tell if the company is basically lying or basically telling the truth.

Ah, but can you *really* tell? All the customer has to go by are bits on a screen. Couldn't a clever marketing person pony up a page that looks hip and happy, successfully masking the cries of anguish coming from the corporate cube farm?

Yes, for a while. Marketing has been training its practitioners for decades in the art of impersonating sincerity and warmth. But marketing can no longer keep up appearances. People talk. They get on the Web and they let the world know that the happy site with the smiling puppy masks a company with coins where its heart is supposed to be. They tell the world that the company that promises to make you feel like royalty doesn't reply to e-mail messages and makes you pay the shipping charges when you return their crappy merchandise. The market will find out who and what you are. Count on it.

That's why you poison your own well when you lie. You break trust with your own people as well as your customers. You *may* be able to win back the trust you've blown, but only by speaking in a real voice, and by engaging people rather than delivering messages to them.

The good news is that almost all of us already know how to talk like real people. It's just a matter of pulling that fat axe from our skulls.

The wrong kind of buzz

*English is the perfect language
for preachers because it allows you to talk
until you think of what to say.*

Garrison Keillor

It's easier to locate and disarm the marketing messages buzzing in our heads than to disable the vocabulary that's been slipped in. At the word level, we all at times slip into the old marketing-speak. Nowhere is this more true than in the technology industries. For example, Bob Epstein, back when he ran Sybase, once gave an otherwise good speech in which he used the expression 'extended enterprise client server'. Afterwards a number of attendees were asked if they could recall this phrase. Most could remember that the phrase was a bunch of buzzwords, but none could remember the phrase itself.

This is because 'extended enterprise client server' is composed entirely of TechnoLatin, a vocabulary of vague but precise-sounding words that work like the blank tiles in Scrabble: you can use them anywhere, but they have no value. TechnoLatin takes perfectly meaningful words and empties them. If language is a living organism, TechnoLatin words are like those pod people in the movie *Invasion of the Body Snatchers*. They look real, but they are not. And like the pod people, TechnoLatin has become the norm. Clarity is the exception when it should be the rule. Today we no longer make chips, circuit boards, computers, monitors or printers. We don't even make products. Instead we make *solutions*, a fatuous noun further bloated by empty modifiers such as *total, full, seamless, industry standard* and *state-of-the-art*.

Equally vague and common are *platform, open, environment* and *support* when used as a verb. A veterinarian using TechnoLatin might say that a dog serves as a platform for sniffing, is an open environment for fleas, and that it supports barking.

This isn't language. It's camouflage.

A perfect example of TechnoLatin's mindless power is a press release that heralded the pointless name change of the semifamiliar Xymos to the anonymous Appian Technology:

> *Over the past two years, Xymos has been repositioning itself. No longer a typical semiconductor supplier, the company has focused on its ability to integrate advanced technologies that use innovative system architecture and software into high performance system solutions for PCs and workstations.*

If communication had taken place here, we would probably know what Appian Technology now does for a living. But because the release is written in TechnoLatin, it offers no such clues. While Xymos was at least 'a typical semiconductor supplier', Appian Technology isn't even a noun. Instead it is 'focused' on an 'ability' to 'integrate' a pod salad of 'advanced technologies', 'innovative system architecture', 'high performance system solutions' and so forth.

Since 'Appian' was first a famous Roman highway, you'd think this might be a clue to Xymos's new identity. But the release says:

> *Appian was chosen for the name because it represents the ability to use leading edge technology and innovation, integrated into solutions that provide differentiation and competitive advantage.*

Just what the Romans had in mind.

The obligatory quote from Appian's president and CEO really hits the nail on the board: 'What we have done at Appian Technology is couple leading-edge technology with innovation, and integrated it into high performance system solutions which provide customers with differentiation and competitive advantage.' This took two years?

Amazingly, Appian Technology did not kill itself. Instead it quietly yawned into a coma. Today its stock maintains a newsless flat line at 1/128th above zero.

It's obvious why we fall into TechnoLatin even if we know better. We sound so smart when we use words no one quite understands. We sound so precise. And we sound like we *belong*: 'distributed platform environment' does for technology marketers what 'you know, like, whatever ...' does for teenagers.

And, of course, it's not just the technology industry that's in love with pod words. Brochureware at **www.ford.com** talks about the Lincoln's 'advanced performance characteristics', 'leading-edge safety systems' and 'AdvanceTrac™ yaw control'. Not to be outdone, Honda says its Odyssey (the car Odysseus would have chosen to drive to Troy, no doubt) has a 'rear crush zone', an 'advanced Traction Control System' and 'Grade Logic programming'. And, of course, restaurants have their own cant (call it GastroFrench, followed by Nouveau GastroFrench), as do interior decorators, sportscasters, Boy Scout leaders, and just about everyone else – loose-limbed phrases that are trotted out as if the real words of the craft were somehow too humble.

So our advice: speak real words. The new Web conversations are remarkably sensitive to the empty pomposity that has served marketing so well. Until now.

Who speaks?

But who gets to speak?

Companies feel a tremendous urge to control communications; it seems as bred-in-the-bone as wanting to sell products. They create organisation charts to define who gets to do the talking. They issue policy statements: only PR can talk to the press. Only Investor Relations can talk to financial folk. Only the CEO can talk to The Journal. We can't afford to muddy our message or dislocate our positioning. God knows what some disgruntled worker might tell valuable customers! So, let's set up a command hierarchy and station it in a hardened communications bunker.

You might as well try to sew closed a fishing net. The simple fact is that your employees are already joining the market conversation. And in most cases it's because they find conversations about what they are working on to be really interesting. They like talking with customers. They like to help. And, sorry to point this out, but they also like complaining if the business is flawed at heart.

The one thing they *don't* want to do, would never do on their own, is deliver a message. And if you make that their role, they will be exposed immediately as company tools. We're all superb at sniffing out the shills: they lack spontaneity, their language is stilted and they are just a little *too* happy. In fact, in Usenet newsgroups, it's not uncommon to find participants being warned about postings from particular people who've blown their credibility by sounding like corporate mouthpieces.

So, what's a business to do? People aren't going to simply repeat messages. You can't shut them up – at least not for long – and you can't make them mouth words they don't believe any more than you could get your teenaged children, your spouse, your friends or *anyone* to. Save your discipline for the few renegades who, through malice or ignorance, spill beans that need to be kept in the can. Expend your efforts instead on building a company that stands for something worthwhile, so that you can't wait to unleash every single one of your voices into the wilds of the new global conversation.

The web of voices

But what about the risk? Suppose a 'lowly clerk' speaks for the company in public and says something wrong? Something actionable? Something confidential, or sensitive? Lordy, what would become of us then?

Let's put this differently: shall we agree to let the sun rise tomorrow? It's going to happen. It already is happening. And it's always happened. The mail clerk describes the corporate strategy to the stranger next to him on the bus, and then provides a critique. The technical-documentation writer tells her cousin how to circumvent the cover-your-ass 'safety' lid. And the telephone support rep tells a customer – on company time! – that one of the features touted on the box doesn't really work exactly as described.

Each of these people is speaking for the company. But, through a game of selective attention, businesses claim their unauthorised personnel aren't really speaking for the company. Not *officially*. Officially there are communication channels that generally correspond to the corporate hierarchy. Officially the entire corporation speaks through a single orifice. Anything that issues from it is sanctioned, true and legally actionable. Anything that does not come through 'approved channels' is just the random lip-flapping of employees for which the corporation is not legally liable.

Of course, all of the excitement, all of the heat, all of the jazz comes from these flapping lips who are speaking for the corporation in everything but the legal sense. They're improvising, not staying 'on message'. They're pursuing the interests they share with the customers, not corporate interests that are at war with customers. Businesses that try to get their people to say exactly the same thing in exactly the same words ('No, Jenkins, for the 100th time, you've left "enhanced" out of "The world's leading manufacturer of enhanced software solutions for maximising supply chain advantage"!') are losing their greatest marketing resource. Now those lips have the global megaphone of the Web. In a Webbed world, loose lips *float* ships.

The people to whom employees are talking and have always talked are sophisticated enough to know that there's a big difference between a Saturn technician answering a customer question in a discussion on the Web and an official reply from Saturn technical support. They know the contents of a press release are not the same as the pep talk that Saturn's president gives at the company picnic. Part of listening to a voice is assessing the role of the words and the speaker. The Web is giving us lots of training in that.

There is, of course, the legal question. While the people engaged in a conversation almost always know precisely the degree of official-ness with which someone is talking, lawyers worry that someone could unintentionally or maliciously take a casual remark as official policy. And of course that could happen. But businesses take legal risks just by shipping products.

For that reason, it'd be good for employees to make every effort to clarify the status of their remarks. No, this does *not* mean that they should sign their e-mail with the phrase 'Does not necessarily represent the views of Management, etc.' – a common sign of worker alienation. The real aim is to communicate the status, not to introduce still more legalisms. Or a business could forbid its employees from talking on the Web during business hours and from identifying themselves as employees after hours. They could build a firewall that – to use the more apt metaphor – turns their company into a black hole on the Web. Of course, the Web conversation would go on without a hiccup. When the company's silence becomes noticeable in some discussion – 'Hey, why doesn't someone from ABC Corp. explain how to keep its product from catching on fire if you put the key in upside down?' – the void will be filled by expert (but exasperated) customers, and then by competitors. If the company truly succeeds in turning itself into a black hole, it may indeed not be talked about on the Web. Or anywhere.

Framejacking

use framejacking to refer to getting contexts radically wrong: throwing rubbish into a litter bin that's for sale in a hardware store, or asking George Clooney to look at your child's rash. Marketing-as-usual has to fight its desire to engage in some serious framejacking on the Web. For example, at a conference, I once heard a representative of a national bank explain with pride that his bank sends out e-mails touting services targeted to particular users, under the signature of the local manager. The messages artfully include typos. And they make sure not to send them out at 2 am since that would strain the credulity of their pigeons, um, customers. This is a distressing spin on '1:1 marketing', a phrase invented by Don Peppers and Martha Rodgers to describe providing personalised offers and services from a mass marketer. Since it's really software that's addressing the '1' customer, this should probably be called 0:1 marketing and, when it pretends to be really 1:1, it's framejacking.

Likewise, personalisation software enables sites to modify what they show you based upon your history of interactions there. This can make a site much more useful to each visitor, but if it tries to make it seem that behind the site is a real human being who loves you for yourself, well, that's some serious framejacking ... and a serious betrayal of trust.

– David Weinberger

There's your risk for you.

On the positive side, by acknowledging that, inevitably, many people speak for a particular company in many different ways, the company can address one of the most important and difficult questions: How can a large company have conversations with hundreds of millions of real people?

First, the conversations don't all have to be truly interactive. Few people insist on personal service immediately from every Web site. We're delighted to look through the Frequently Asked Questions (FAQs) and ReadMe files to find our answers – answers culled from the real interactions between the company and its market.

When a conversation is required, or even just desired, being able to count upon a rich range of corporate spokespeople is crucial. That's the only way a growing business can satisfy the market's demand for conversation. For example, at Western Digital's Web site (**http://www.wdc.com**), users can post technical questions about the company's hard disk drives. Most of those questions are, naturally, about drives that don't work. A Western Digital support person will post an answer, often within hours, and the entire exchange is open to public view, unfiltered. As a result, customers with problems can usually find a previous exchange that answers their questions. Sure, visitors to the

Robo-Voice

Technology is clearing away some of the non-conversational conversations we used to have: 'Hello. How are you? Fine, thanks. What can I do for you today? Is that it then? OK, you have a good day' repeated 12 times an hour, 40 hours a week. An ATM will do just fine, thanks. Yes, we lose some human contact, and there are certainly places where the brief dialogue with the bank teller is part of a social fabric that shouldn't be sundered – part of the ancient marketplace that has survived. If that's true for you, then you'll avoid ATMs. But in many instances, automated transactions are liberating people from semi-automatic human behaviours.

In other cases, the automation afforded by the Web is *increasing* the quality of offline marketplaces. For example, in part to compete with Amazon.com, local bookstores are enhancing their conversational accoutrements, and many of us appreciate them all the more precisely because of the 'frictionless' ease of acquiring books from Amazon.

site find out that not all Western Digital drives work flawlessly forever, but this is hardly a news flash. More important, they learn that Western Digital has enough confidence in its products to let customers air their gripes, and that if a drive breaks, it'll get diagnosed and fixed at the speed of the Web. And, perhaps most important, they see that the company's customers and enthusiasts care enough to dive in. Could a company ask for better living testimonials? Could customers ask for a livelier, more reality-based source of information?

If you want to hear the sound of the new marketing, listen to these conversations coming from inside, outside, over and above even the hardest-shelled companies that still think marketing means lobbing messages into crowds. Here is the same sound our ancestors heard in those ancient marketplaces, where people spoke for themselves about what mattered to them.

How to talk

We're all learning to talk anew. We're all going to get it right *and* get it wrong. Two events in the autumn of 1994 still serve as good cases in point for crisis management. In one case, resolute Ivory Tower isolation caused a major disaster. In the other, real conversation among concerned individuals saved the day.

First, an anatomy of a disaster. Through the 1980s and early 1990s, Compuserve hosted many of the best online forums. One of these professional salons was the *EETimes* Forum, hosted by *Electronic Engineering Times*, the top magazine for the people who design and work with computer chips. It's a safe bet that most of the participants used Intel-based computers, and engineered computers with 'Intel Inside'. Yet when news of a bug in an early Pentium chip was first found and posted on the forum, nobody seemed to take it too seriously. They joked about it a bit, but took it in their stride. After all, bugs in chips are nothing new. But all of them clearly were looking for Intel to jump in and talk about it.

However, there was radio silence from Intel until Alex Wolfe, an *EETimes* reporter, wrote about the bug in his magazine. Soon the major media picked up the story and all hell broke loose.

To deal with this crisis, Intel CEO Andy Grove posted something on the forum that read like a papal encyclical on how Intel works. This included a description of a caste system that drew a line between those who should be concerned about such a bug and those who should not, and offered to replace the defective chips for the first group. This didn't sit well with anybody, but the forum members were tolerant at first. They wanted to get to the bottom of this thing, so they attempted to engage Grove on the matter. After all, he had showed up. He must have been willing to talk. But it quickly became obvious that Grove was just posting a notice – the big guy was not going to take part in a conversation.

So, when Intel got shellacked in the press, little help came from what should have been company friends in the engineering community. After all, these were Intel's real customers. They understood how bugs happen. They were articulate and authoritative. But they were just as silent for Grove as Grove had been for them. Intel was publicly embarrassed into recalling every one of the defective chips, and estimates for reputation damage ran into many millions.

Meanwhile, over in Compuserve's Travel Forum, another bad PR event was taking shape. This one involved United Airlines, which was experiencing a bumpy take-off with its new Shuttle By United service. Like the *EETimes* Forum, the Travel Forum had serious participants: high-mileage fliers, pilots, air traffic controllers, travel agents and airline personnel from every level.

If you could hook up a meter to the forum and measure good will, the needle reading for Shuttle By United at take-off was way over on the negative side. Luggage was being lost (three times for one passenger). Passenger loading was chaotic. Customers were unhappy.

Then one United worker (one of those 'owners' United's ads talked about so much at the time) jumped in and simply started to help out. The response was remarkable. Here are a few examples:

> **'Good to see someone at United interested!'**
>
> **'Nice to have a UAL person to chat with ... thanks.'**
>
> **'As a 100k flier, I'm glad to see one of you online here.'**

> 'I am a pilot for United and I thank you for taking the time to answer all of
> these questions about the Shuttle.'
>
> 'Nice to see a UA employee on and participating instead of just lurking.'
>
> 'As a UA 1K FF [top-grade frequent flyer] and a PassPlus holder I appreciate
> your time and interest in the forum.'
>
> 'Don't leave United. You're important to us. Your comments are helpful. You
> make a difference.'

This kind of conversation moved the meter all the way over to the positive side, just
because one company guy took on the burden of talking with customers and trying
to solve their problems. *One guy*.

Then one day the same UA employee posted a notice that said, 'Due to a conflict
with corporate communication policies at United Airlines of employees responding
to issues of any nature without the explicit direction of the Communications
Division, I will not be participating any longer. I hope this situation changes in the
future. Until then, direct any concerns to the Consumer Affairs department at
United's World Headquarters.'

You can imagine what followed. United got flamed royally by their employee's new
friends on the forum.

But, unlike Intel, United stayed in the conversation. A United higher-up jumped in
and quickly communicated United's willingness to learn this new form of market
relations. The original United correspondent and the higher-up both stayed in the
conversation and started to work things out. The needle went back over to the
positive side. And nobody ever heard bad news about the Shuttle by United bug.

Lessons learned? The party's already started. You can join or not. If you don't, your
silence will be taken as arrogance, stupidity, meanness, or all three. If you're going
to join, don't do it as a legal entity or wearing your cloak of officialdom. Join it as a
person with a name, a point of view, a sense of humour, and passion.

Marketing craft

The market started out as a place where people talked about what they cared about, in voices as individual as the craft goods on the table between them. As the distance between producer and consumer lengthened, so grew the gap between our business voice and our authentic voice. Marketing became a profession, an applied science, the engineering of desirable responses through the application of calibrated stimuli – including the occasional axe in the head.

Marketing isn't going to go away. Nor should it. But it needs to evolve, rapidly and thoroughly, for markets have become networked and now know more than business, learn faster than business, are more honest than business, and are a hell of a lot more fun than business. The voices are back, and voice brings craft: work by unique individuals motivated by passion.

What's happening to the market is precisely what should – and will – happen to marketing. Marketing needs to become a craft. Recall that craftworkers listen to the material they're forming, shaping the pot to the feel of the clay, designing the house to fit with and even reveal the landscape. The stuff of marketing is the market itself. Marketing can't become a craft until it can hear the new – the old – sound of its markets.

By listening, marketing will re-learn how to talk.

C H A P T E R

The hyperlinked organisation

DAVID WEINBERGER

BUSINESS SOUNDS DIFFERENT THESE DAYS.

The words at meetings have an edge. The language used with customers is unfiltered. The e-mails are pithy, often piercing.

Where once bombastic self-confidence got you taken seriously, now being funny does.

In fact, there's laughter everywhere, although it signals insight and bitterness as often as delight.

Sometimes you could swear you hear children's laughter in the background, over the sounds of cooking and cockatiels and the UPS truck arriving.

Beneath the formalities of business – the committees, the schedules, the payroll checks, the spray of assignments falling from above – there's a buzz, no, the sound of twigs breaking underfoot as paths are trod on the way to human connection. The most amazing thing: you can tell who's talking by listening to the voice.

People are beginning to sound like themselves again.

Intranet apocalypso

You may not hear any of this at your place of work. But if the Web has touched your business – and it has – then the sound is there.

The odd thing is that you almost certainly have to be making some of the new sound to hear it. Otherwise, it passes for noise, like an overtone of the 60-cycle thrum of modern business at its automated, time-slicing best.

You hear it or you don't. You get it or you don't. The gulf that has opened in companies is about the size of the human heart.

That's what makes the situation so ripe for humour. And anger. And absurdity.

Consider this: from the other side of the gulf opened by the Web, virtually all of the structures that management identifies as being the business itself seem to be bizarre artifacts of earlier times, like wearing a powdered wig and codpiece to the company picnic.

The gulf the Web opens is, ironically, that of connection. Without anyone asking for it, the Web has given the people inside an organisation easy access to one another in a rich variety of ways. They can send e-mail to one person, to a steady group, to a dynamic team, to the entire sales force, or 'just' to the board of directors. They can post creative, informative pages that express their interests, correct the mistakes in the official technical documentation, or point to the industry analyst's report the company doesn't want anyone to read. They can write a 'zine that parodies the company line savagely and without let-up. They can play backgammon online or blow up their colleagues in a ruthless game of Quake in which the guy who never speaks at meetings routinely turns his manager into animated meat chunks. They can also find every piece of information about the company and its competitors, shop for a car or learn how to play the blues like Buddy Guy.

The Web, in short, has led every wired person in your organisation to expect direct connections not only to information but also to the truth spoken in human voices. And they expect to be able to find what they need and do what they need without any further help from people who dress better than they do. This has happened not because of a management theory or a bestselling business book but because the Web reaches everyone with a computer and a telephone line on their desk.

So, the gulf opens between those who are connected and those who think an office with a door is a sign of success. The gulf is one of expectations, and expectations always guide perception. As a result, the company thinks it's doing one thing while accomplishing the direct opposite with its connected employees. For example:

- The company **communicates** with me through a newsletter and company meetings meant to lift up my morale. In fact, I know from my e-mail pen pals that it's telling me happy-talk lies, and I find that quite depressing.

- The company **organisation chart** shows me who does what so I know how to get things done. In fact, the organisation chart is an expression of a power structure. It is red tape. It is a map of whom to avoid.

- The company **manages my work** to make sure that all tasks are co-ordinated and the company is operating efficiently. In fact, the inflexible goals imposed from on high keep me from following what my craft expertise tells me I really ought to be doing.

- The company provides me with a **career path** so I'll see a productive future in the business. In fact, I've figured out that because the organisation chart narrows at the top, most career paths necessarily have to be dead ends.

- The company provides me with all the **information** I need to make good decisions. In fact, this information is selected to support a decision (or worldview) in which I have no investment. Statistics and industry surveys are lobbed like anti-aircraft fire to disguise the fact that while we have lots of data, we have no understanding.

- The company is **goal-oriented** so that the path from here to there is broken into small, well-marked steps that can be tracked and managed. In fact, if I keep my head down and accomplish my goals, I won't add the type of value I'm capable of. I need to browse. I even need to play. Without play, only Shit Happens. With play, Serendipity Happens.

- The company gives me **deadlines** so that we ship product on time, maintaining our integrity. In fact, working to arbitrary deadlines makes me ship poor-quality content. My management doesn't have to use a club to get me to do my job. Where's the trust, baby?

- The company looks at **customers** as adversaries who must be won over. In fact, the ones I've been exchanging e-mail with are very cool and enthusiastic about exactly the same thing that got me into this company. You know, I'd rather talk with them than with my manager.

- The company works in an **office building** in order to bring together all of the things I need to get my job done and to avoid distracting me. In fact, more and more of what I need is outside the corporate walls. And when I *really* want to get something done, I go home.

- The company rewards me for being a **professional** who acts and behaves in a, well, professional manner, following certain unwritten rules about the coefficient of permitted variation in dress, politics, shoe style, expression of religion and the relating of humourous stories. In fact, I learn who to trust – whom I can work with creatively and productively – only by getting past the professional act.

Something's gone wrong. Or maybe something now is starting to go right.

What's wrong isn't trivial. It isn't fixed with dress-down Fridays, health food in the cafeteria, or learning to pretend to look into the eyes of the trembling subordinate you're condescending to chat up on the way in from the parking lot. The power structure, the politics, the sociology, even the spirituality of work has a sick, sour smell to it.

But you don't need big words. It all begins with pictures. That's why our hairy-backed ancestors were sketching bison on the wall: they were learning to see. So let's think instead about the basic *picture* we have of business.

Inside fort business

Somewhere along the line, we confused going to work with building a fort.

Strip away the financial jibber-jabber and the management corpo-speak, and here's our fundamental image of business:

- It's in an imposing office building that towers over the landscape.
- Inside is everything we need.
- And that's good because the outside is dangerous. We are under siege by our

competitors, and even by our partners and customers. Thank God for the thick, high walls!

- The king rules. If we have a wise king, we prosper.

- The king has a court. The dukes, viscounts and other subluminaries each receive their authority from the king. (The king even countenances an official fool. Within limits.)

- We each have our role, our place. If we each do the job assigned to us by the king's minions, our fort will beat all those other stinking forts.

- And then we will have succeeded – or, thinking it's the same thing, we will say we have 'won'. We get to dance a stupid jig while chanting 'Number one! Number one!'

This fort is, at its heart, a place apart. We report there every morning and spend the next 8, 10, or 12 hours inaccessible to the 'real' world. The portcullis drops not only to keep out our enemies, but to separate us from distractions such as our families. As the drawbridge goes up behind us, we become business people, different enough from our normal selves that when we first bring our children to the office, they've been known to hide under our desk, crying.

Within this world, the Web looks like a medium that exists to allow Fort Business to publish online marketing materials and make credit card sales easier than ever. Officially, this point of view is known as 'denial'.

The Web isn't primarily a medium for information, marketing or sales. It's a world in which people meet, talk, build, fight, love and play. In fact, the Web world is bigger than the business world and is swallowing the business world whole. The vague rumblings you're hearing are the sounds of digestion.

The change is so profound that it's not merely a negation of the current situation. You can't just put a big 'not' in front of Fort Business and say, 'Ah, the walls are coming down.' No, the true opposite of a fort isn't an unwalled city.

It's a conversation.

Hyperlinks subvert hierarchy

Fort Business's assumptions are being challenged by a meek little thing: a hyperlink.

How could something so small alter the fundamentals of business life? Easy. This wee beastie represents an important change in how pieces are put together – and since all of life is about putting pieces together, this isn't a wee thing at all.

Sure, businesses are legal entities. But that's just a piece of paper. In fact, the real business is the set of connections among people.

Modern business almost universally has chosen a particular type of togetherness: a hierarchy. There are two distinguishing marks of a hierarchy: it has a top and a bottom, and the top is narrower than the bottom. Power flows from the top and there are fewer and fewer people as you move up the food chain.

This not only makes the line of authority crystal clear, it also enhances the allure of success by making it into an exclusive club. As La Rochefoucauld once said, 'It is not enough that I succeed. It is also necessary that my friends fail.'

No wonder so many of us stare at our bare feet in the morning and wonder why we're putting on our socks.

A couple of other points about business hierarchies:

First, they assume – along with Ayn Rand and poorly socialised adolescents – that the fundamental unit of life is the individual. This is despite the evidence of our senses that individuals only emerge from groups – groups like families and communities. (You know, it really does take a village to raise a child. Just like it takes a corporation to raise an ass kisser.)

Understanding through hyperlinks

Ever since Aristotle, we understand what something is by seeing what category it's in and how it differs from other things in that category. For example, humans are in the category of animals, but we are the rational ones. This knowledge hierarchy constrains things to a single category. In a hyperlinked world, however, things can be understood by reference (via metaphor) to other things – and can be like more than one thing at a time.

If you change the way we understand things, you've changed something very significant indeed.

But the Web obviously isn't predicated on individuals. It's a web. It's about the connections. And on the World Wide Web, the connections are hyperlinks. It's not just documents that get hyperlinked in the new world of the Web. People do. Organisations do. The Web, in the form of a corporate intranet, puts everyone in touch with every piece of information and with everyone else inside the organisation and beyond.

The potential connections are vast. Hyperlinks are the connections made by real individuals based on what they care about and what they know, the paths that emerge because that's where the feet are walking, as opposed to the highways bulldozed into existence according to a centralised plan.

Hyperlinks have no symmetry, no plan. They are messy. More can be added, old ones can disappear, and nothing else has to change. Compare this to your latest reorganisation where you sat down with the organisation chart and your straight edge and worried about holes and imbalances and neatness for heaven's sake! A messy organisation chart is the devil's playground, after all.

Second, business hierarchies are power structures only because fundamentally they're based on fear.

Organisation charts are pyramids. The ancient pharaohs built their pyramids out of the fear of human mortality. Today's business pharaohs build their pyramidal organisations out of fear of human fallibility; they're afraid of being exposed as frightened little boys, fallible and uncertain.

To be human is to be imperfect. We die. We make mistakes.

Sometimes we run from our fallibility by being decisive. But doubt is the natural human state, and decisiveness – more addictive than anything you might shoot into your veins – is often based on a superstitious belief in the magic of action.

Within the pyramid we have defined roles and responsibilities. We tell ourselves that this is so the business will run efficiently, but in fact having a role brings us the great comfort of having a turf where we're pretty confident we're not going to be shown up … except maybe by that ambitious jerk on the fourth floor, but we've figured out a way to hook his brains out through his nose, which should delay him at least for a little while.

Of course, dividing the business up into fanatically defended turfs doesn't really protect anyone from fallibility and uncertainty, the very things that mark us as humans.

So, here's some news for today's business pharaohs: your pyramid is being replaced by hyperlinks. It was built on sand anyway.

The Web liberates business from the fear of being exposed as human, even against its will. It throws everyone into immediate connection with everyone else without the safety net of defined roles and authorities, but it also sets the expectation that you'll make human-size mistakes rather frequently. Now that you've lost the trappings of authority, and you find yourself standing next to the junior graphic designer for gawd's sake, and you can't hide behind your business card, what the hell are you going to do?

You're going to talk with her. You're going to have a conversation. And if you harrumph and try to make sure she knows that you're Very Important by the power vested in you by the power that vested in you, well, she's going to laugh once out loud and five times in e-mail and tell everyone else what an asshole you are.

You see, the hyperlinks that replace the organisation chart as the primary structure of the organisation are in fact conversations. They are the paths talk takes. And a business is, more than anything else, the set of conversations going on.

Business is a conversation because the defining work of a business is conversation – literally. And 'knowledge workers' are simply those people whose job consists of having interesting conversations.

'Can I super-size that?' 'Have it on my desk by the morning', 'There's no *I* in Team', and laughing at your manager's unfunny jokes are not conversations. Conversations are where ideas happen and partnerships are formed. Sometimes they create commitments (in Fernando Flores' sense), but more often they're pulling people through fields of common interest with no known destination. The structure of conversations is always hyperlinked and is never hierarchical:

> To have a conversation, you have to be comfortable being human – acknowledging you don't have all the answers, being eager to learn from someone else and to build new ideas together.

> You can only have a conversation if you're not afraid to be wrong. Otherwise, you're not conversing, you're just declaiming, speechifying, or reading what's on the PowerPoints. To converse, you have to be willing to be wrong in front of another person.

> Conversations occur only between equals. The time your boss's boss asked you at a meeting about your project's deadline was not a conversation. The time you sat with your boss's boss for an hour in the Polynesian-themed bar while on a business trip and you really talked, got past the corporate bullshit, told each other the truth about the dangers ahead, and ended up talking about your kids – that maybe was a conversation.

Conversations subvert hierarchy. Hyperlinks subvert hierarchy. Being a human being among others subverts hierarchy.

Bottom-up

The Web is undoubtedly a part of your business plans. You've got it safely contained, under control, managed. Why, your organisation has probably already installed a corporate intranet so it can publish the human resource policies that no one read on paper to people who now won't read 'em on screen. Excellent!

Yes, your centralised corporate intranet has eliminated some paper and is making management feel vaguely cool. But that's not the web that's going to shake the foundations of your fort.

While you've been hiring consultants to create a slick corporate intranet, establishing policies about who gets to post what, and creating a chain of command to ensure that only appropriate and approved materials show up on your internal corporate home page, your engineers, scientists, researchers – hell even the marketing folks – have been creating little Web sites for their own use.

No one is controlling what's posted on them except the people doing the posting. No one is making sure that the corporate logo is in the right place. No one is making sure that the writing is official, officious and as dull as the pencil drawer of a recently downsized middle manager.

The real party got under way while you were still setting up the banners at the corporate prom. (This year's prom theme: 'Responsibility in a Web Age!')

For example, by the time Sun Microsystems got around to counting, they had 800 intranets. And when Texas Instruments put in their corporate intranet, they invited everyone who had one already in place to register with the top-down one. Within a few months, 250 internal sites had registered, and no one knows how many unregistered ones there were. Even a top-down intranet can take on a bottom-up feel, as happened at Lucent Technologies, according to an article in The Wall Street Journal. After Lucent brought together a product-development team of 500 engineers across 3 continents and 13 time zones, it watched dozens of them insert their own pages into the project intranet. Some of these pages related directly to the project; others were strictly personal, like, 'Hey, look at this picture of me and my dog!' Either way, the project took on a human cast that never would have been present otherwise. In the end the team leader attributed the success of the project in no small part to 'the ultimate Democracy of the Web'.

Granted, these are technology companies, but you don't have to be a technical genius to create an intranet. If someone wants to share some information, they can turn their computer into a Web server. It's free, and it's getting easier every day.

The intranet revolution is bottom-up. There's no going back. If a company doesn't recognise this, the top-down intranet it puts in can breed the type of cynicism that results in ugly bathroom graffiti and mysterious golfing cart accidents.

The intranets under the radar screen – and the rest of the Net panoply, including e-mail, mailing lists and discussion groups – ignore the corporate blather and ass-covering pronouncements. Instead, these new Web conversations are actually being used to get some work done.

The character of the Web

It's weird, but not totally unexpected.

It turns out that the Web is infecting organisations with the characteristics of its own architecture. So, if you want to know what a hyperlinked organisation looks like, look at what the Web itself is like.

What's the Web's character? You can slice it into seven basic themes:

1. **Hyperlinked.** Before the Web, computer networks were laid out in advance like well-planned cities. Who got connected to whom and how was all part of the master plan. And once you were connected, there was a recognisable central authority responsible for the whole shebang. The Web isn't even a little like that. The Web literally consists of hundreds of millions of pages hyperlinked together by the author of each individual page. Anyone can plug in and any page can be linked to any other, without asking permission. The Web is constantly spinning itself – many small pieces loosely joining themselves as they see fit.

2. **Decentralised.** No one is in charge of the Net. There is no central clearing house that dispatches all requests and approves all submissions. No one ordered the Web built. There is no CEO of the Web. There is no one to sue. There's no one to complain to. There's no one to fix it when it breaks. There's no one to thank.

3. **Hyper time.** Internet time is, famously, seven times the velocity of 'normal' time. And yet we use the leisurely verb *browse* to describe our behaviour on the Web because in the virtual world, I feel I can move about at my own pace, exploring when and where I want. I can take a quick look at a site and come back later without having to find another parking space, go to the end of the line, or pay a second entry fee. The Web puts the control of my time into my hands.

4. **Open, direct access.** The Net provides what feels like direct access to everyone else on the Net and to every piece of information that's ever been posted. If you want to go to a page, you just click on the link and, boom, you're there. (The fact that this might have required, beneath the surface, 30 'hops' among servers in places you never heard of is completely irrelevant. You don't see the hops; you just see the page.) There's nothing standing between you and the rest of the world of people and pages.

5. **Rich data.** The currency of the Web isn't green bar printouts of facts and stats. It's pages. Humans have been creating pages since the invention of paper and dirty water. Pages – or 'documents' as we sometimes say – are extraordinarily complex ways of presenting information. Typically, they tell you as much about the author as about their topic, a big change from the pre-Web information environment that aimed at generating faceless data.

6. **Broken.** Because the Web is by far the largest, most complex network ever built, and because no one owns it or controls it, it is always going to be, in the words of Tim Berners-Lee, the inventor of the Web, 'a little bit broken'.

7. **Borderless.** Because traditional networks were concerned as much with security as with access, it was usually made clear where your stuff ended and other people's stuff began. The Web, on the other hand, was designed so that you can include a link to a page without having to get the author's permission. Thus, on the Web it is often hard to tell exactly where the boundaries are.

From these characteristics of the technical architecture of the Web come the changes that are transforming your business.

The hyperlinking of the organisation

Your organisation is becoming hyperlinked. Whether you like it or not. It's bottom-up; it's unstoppable.

Despite the wet stink of fear, you ought to be delighted. Hyperlinked organisations are closer to their markets, act faster and acquire the valuable survival skill of learning to swerve.

Of course, they also are impossible to manage – although they can be 'unmanaged'—and you'll have to give up your pretence of power, status and lordliness. But, then, as the old saying has it, you can't make an omelet without nuking the existing social order.

Here's the drill for the rest of this chapter. We've just discussed seven key characteristics of the Web. Now we're going to go through them one at a time, in order (no talking in the hallways and please stand to the right to enable those in a hurry to pass) to see what's happening inside organisations touched by the Web – that is, all organisations to one degree or another.

Let's put the hyper back into hyperlinks

Here's one example of how things work in a hyperlinked organisation:

> You're a sales rep in the Southwest who has a customer with a product problem. You know that the Southwest tech-support person happens not to know anything about this problem. In fact, she's a flat-out bozo. So, to do what's right for your customer you go outside the prescribed channels and pull together the support person from the Northeast, a product manager you respect, and a senior engineer who's been responsive in the past (no good deed goes unpunished!). Via e-mail or by building a mini-Web site on an intranet, you initiate a discussion, research numbers, check out competitive solutions and quickly solve the customer's problem – all without ever notifying the 'appropriate authorities' of what you're doing because all they'll do is try to force you back into the official channels.

It's a little thing. But it's a big change in the ground rules of work. The official structure is of little use to you. Instead, your network of trusted colleagues becomes paramount. Your effectiveness depends upon how networked you are, how hyperlinked you are.

The hyperlinked teams you form may not be as project-centred as in the example above. As organisations become hyperlinked, they spawn hyperlinked committees, hyperlinked task forces, hyperlinked affiliations, hyperlinked interest groups, hyperlinked communities, hyperlinked cheering squads, hyperlinked pen pals and hyperlinked attitudes. Humans seem to fill up every available social niche just as nature itself abhors an ecological vacuum.

These hyperlinked relationships are, like the Web of hyperlinked documents, a shifting context of links of varying importance and quality. They are self-asserting, not requiring anyone else's authority to be put in place. And the value of the individual 'node' to a large degree depends upon the node's links.

This last point is a big shift. Links have value by pointing *away* from themselves to some other site. All Web pages derive *some* value from the links on them. (A page with no links is literally a dead end on the Web.) In fact, the single most-visited site on the Web, Yahoo!, derives almost all of its value not from what it contains but from what it points to. Yet our understanding of the nature of knowledge, education and expertise is bound up with things that *contain* value, not with things that point you out of themselves to find value elsewhere. Books get their value from their content. Education is the transfer of content into the receptacle that is the student. And an expert is someone who contains a lot of information, like a book contains information. In fact, experts are people who can write books. But, with today's huge increase in the amount of information, you can be an expert only in something sliced so thin that often it's trivial. Increasingly, a *useful* expert is not someone with (containing) all the answers but someone who knows where to find answers. The new experts have value not by centralising information and control but by being great 'pointers' to other people and to useful, current information.

In short, your most valuable employee is likely to be the one who, in response to a question, doesn't give a concrete answer in a booming voice but who says, 'You should talk to Larry. And check Janis's project plan. Oh, and there's a mailing list on this topic I ran into a couple of weeks ago ...'

How could you hope to capture this on an organisation chart? And how do you compensate people fairly if their value depends upon their participation in a shifting set of hyperlinked associations? How do you hire great hyperlinked people? How could this ever be expressed on a résumé?

Great questions ... because there aren't clear answers yet. Epochal changes are not Q&A sessions. We're at the beginning of the biggest Q since the Industrial Revolution. It's a time to make things up, try them out, fail a thousand times, and laugh at how stupid you look.

The urge to 'solve the problem' is nothing but the voice of the old command-and-control psychosis trying to reassert itself.

('Premature elucidation': the plight of men who come to answers way too soon.)

Decentralising the fort

Traditionally, business is an indoor sport.

Businesses by their very nature are centralised (or so we think). Even if you are a global enterprise, your organisation consists of a headquarters with regional offices. A business is, after all, a bringing together of talented people who agree to work to achieve some common goals. We've assumed that 'together' means we have to centralise power, control and resources. But there are lots of ways to be together.

Metaphorical togetherness

We often assume that complex projects can only be accomplished through centralised planning and control. It worked for building the Hoover Dam, after all. Not to mention World War II.

But, of course, it only works for some types of wars in some types of places. And the builders of the Hoover Dam aimed at creating a massive physical object with delicate dependencies so that there was only one way to succeed and many ways to fail.

A marriage is a far more complex project than any business partnership, and centralised control doesn't work real well there. Raising a family is likewise a complex project that cannot be centrally organised or planned. And, of course, the most complex network ever imagined – the World Wide Web – has been implemented without any central control whatsoever.

But is a business more like a family than a war? Absolutely. Wars are won and then are over, but companies don't declare victory and disband the troops. And although both wars and companies have missions, companies don't ever issue a press release that says:

> OmniCo is proud to announce that on 23 June we accomplished our mission of being the world's leading supplier of low-temperature oil to the miniature locomotive industry, so we are now demobilising so that our brave men and women can rejoin their families. Good night and God bless.

No, families and businesses are open-ended commitments.

Suppose running a business is more like farming than like waging war. Perhaps the real aim of business is to build a place that provides a high yield over the long term, responding to the sometimes vast changes in the environment.

Command and control don't work when you're cultivating the wilderness, when you're experiencing an ecology of surplus, when changes happen faster than response times, when you're homesteading, not marching to battle. Why is it even necessary to have to point out something so obvious?

That's not a rhetorical question. We all know enough about the inequities of history to smell something suspicious about the insistence on centralised control. Control and management are the mantras of the people who are in power, who judge personal success by power, and who use power to keep themselves at the top.

Organisation charts are written by the victors. But hyperlinks are created by people finding other people they trust, enjoy and, yes, in some ways love.

Self-reliance

In a decentralised environment, people figure out that they have to do things themselves. Indeed, they *want* to do things themselves.

This is a well-known phenomenon in customer support: people would rather find the answers themselves on your Web site than have the answers delivered to them by picking up the phone. This may sound like a control issue, but in fact it is about time. By browsing your support Web site, not only can I choose when I'm going to look and how long before I'll give up, I can click through some screens, work on something else, eat lunch, maybe even bookmark the page, and come back to it tomorrow. I can complete the task on my own schedule.

It shouldn't be surprising that self-reliance is high up in the list of Top Ten Web Virtues. The Web itself started out as a huge do-it-yourself project, and being able to do your own technical support is a mark of Web competency still. More and more, employees and customers want to feel their own hands on the wheel.

Another obvious example: In the old days, if you wanted to find some information, you had to go to the corporate Information Retrieval Expert and fill out a form. But now the Web has reset expectations. If the data hierophants tell you that you're not trained enough to search the corporate library, you'll reply, 'Hey, I just came back from AltaVista' – or Excite or Hotbot or any of the myriad of search sites – 'and I searched through hundreds of millions of pages without any training.'

It's time to hand over the keys to the index. Baby's learned to drive.

Self-reliance, however, goes far beyond the technical realm. For example, Boeing enables mechanics to order parts themselves (through their cleverly named Part Analysis and Requirement Tracking – PARTS – system), instead of petitioning the Purchasing department. And Chrysler encourages employees to make their own travel arrangements via an intranet site that shows them only the appropriate choices (for example, the Concorde doesn't show up as a possibility), saving administrative costs and giving the workers a greater sense (illusion?) of control.

There's a dark side to self-reliance. It can encourage a type of arrogant cynicism that reacts to anything that the business tries to do for you with: 'I can do it better than

> ## Mission statements
>
> Mission statements are directed to customers and prospects – that's why they don't contain the words 'and make us filthy rich' – but they're also part of a conceptual hierarchy that mirrors the power hierarchy (excuse me, organisation chart). At the top is the mission statement. And it begat the strategy. And the strategy begat the tactics. And the tactics begat the objectives that begat the tasks that begat the people in cubicles who no longer beget children because they're working all weekend trying to finish the !@#$-ing assignments they've been given to serve the all-powerful mission statement. If you want to know where to find the real corporate point of view and values, look to the stories that are told off hours when folks are 'just talking'. In short, at the strategic off-site where you're drafting your new mission statement, if you're given a choice between bringing in a consultant or beer, choose the beer.

that.' In this view of the world, there's what I can do with my own two hands and then there's red tape. To the Web cult of self-reliance, the business is not only an obstacle, it's them, the other.

Yet if we know that routing a customer comment through the standard structures of the Fort will result in a content-free form letter being sent out six weeks later, we will sit down and bang out an e-mail immediately that actually addresses the customer's concern. Self-reliance breeds disengagement with the business but more direct engagement with the real work of business.

We are seeing, then, a realignment of loyalties, from resting comfortably in the assumed paternalism of Fort Business to an aggressive devotion to making life better for customers. The business isn't a machine any more, it's a resource I alone and we together can use to make a customer happy.

Hyper time

We all know that Internet time is seven times the speed of normal time. ('On the Internet, everyone knows you don't have time to spellcheck.') It affects our business expectations for Internet startups and our expectations about the quality of products we know have been rushed to market, but there's actually more at stake. In fact, the philosopher Martin Heidegger had it right when he explained that time is at the root of all that is.

Business likes to think that it operates on a master schedule that devolves into lots of supporting schedules, just as the corporate strategy devolves into objectives and then into tasks, and just as the organisation chart foliates into branches, twigs and finally leaves. In a perfectly run business, all the schedules tick in sync. Tick tock tick tock.

Now, we all know that no complex organisation works perfectly, so with a knowing smile we dismiss the possibility – but yet we hold it out as an ideal. Our clocks are supposed to be driven from on high.

The Web decentralises time by letting hyperlinked groups form that are driven by

To: self@evident.com
From: clocke@panix.com

You write: 'The business isn't a machine any more, it's a resource, stuff that I alone and we together can use to make a customer happy.'

I'm always a little bothered by this making-customers-happy trope. Is this *really* why people try harder in orgs? I tend to doubt it. Maybe it's just me, but I don't think people are too often inspired by customers – that's usually just more happy talk.

Instead workers go the extra mile because *they* want to do a good job. To me, pride of craftsmanship is a far greater motivator. If I'm interacting with a customer, I want to show that other *person* that *I* am a professional even if the rest of the company is going to hell in a handbasket.

And I think this is true right up to the level of the CEO.

If you, David Weinberger, want to make your customers happy, I'd say it's more to demonstrate that you're a capable dude – not because you're concerned for your client's mental state.

To: clocke@panix.com
From: self@evident.com

I think we're probably both right (yech). Having customers who are happy to your face is a very big turn-on for a lot of people. You can say that that's only because ultimately it makes *me* feel competent, but you could reduce *all* human actions to that and thus obliterate the real distinction between stealing candy from a baby and devoting your life to working with the poor.

their do-it-ourselves zeal to get stuff done now. For these groups, schedules are driven locally, not centrally. The schedules are created by local groups and individuals, accounting for their assessment of what's realistic. And they route around obstacles, not like building straight-line motorways where it's assumed that all boulders can be blasted out of the way.

Deadlines

But what happens to deadlines if time becomes decentralised?

Let me give you an example that I recount with little pride. I was working in a relatively small software company that was, happily, experiencing growing pains as we went from $3 million to $40 million in revenues. I had been one of the three members of the executive management team that had agreed to roll the dice that set us off on the steep growth curve. My role was strategist. I was never much of an implementer. But because we now desperately needed to run marketing programmes, I agreed to step into the role of VP of Marketing. A couple of months later, we hired a Chief Operating Officer (COO) to manage our growth. On purpose he was a counter-cultural figure in the company: a hard-bitten, ultra-realistic guy with a relentlessly positive attitude applied as a fresco to mask a cracking wall of disagreeable fear.

A couple of weeks after arriving, he called me into his office to bond with me and also, not incidentally, to find out when the next wave of marketing materials would be ready. I said I didn't know. Why not? he demanded. I replied that I had a really well-motivated team of professionals who were moving heaven and earth to get it all done; it would be done at the earliest possible moment.

He looked at me in amazement. And gave up on me.

Now, I will admit that as COO, he needed to have some sense of the timing of events. For example, he might have needed to know when the materials would be ready because of an upcoming sales meeting. And in such a case I would have told him what I thought would be ready. And if he wanted it sooner, I would have warned him that some of it would be of poor quality. But, in fact, there was no upcoming event. He managed by holding people to deadlines. I managed by holding people to people.

His view of me, to this day, is that I am an unrealistic, soft-edged, namby-pamby, probably borderline homosexual type of guy. My view of him is that he's an unrealistic, anal-retentive, power-driven, frightened little boy. (You know, but underneath it all, we actually don't like each other.)

Is one of us more realistic than the other? I don't think so. If not living by deadlines is unrealistic, it's just as unrealistic to think that a motivated group of people, working hard, will get things done by a particular moment just because you set that moment as the endpoint.

Clearly there's room for both personality types (gosh, I am namby-pamby, aren't I?), but since the deadline drivers always get to state their point of view, let's for once not assume that deadlines are the only way to manage, and that people who miss deadlines are like dawdling children who need to be sent to the corner of the organisation chart where they can sit to think about what they've done.

Instead, let's leave open the possibility that deadlines are frequently a weapon used by managers who assume that workers are basically slackers. In fact, hyperlinked teams – ruled by the laws of connection – are motivated by a genuine desire to turn out a product or help a customer. They will work as hard as they can to do right by their customers and their co-workers. They know better than anyone, in many instances, when the work can realistically be finished. Managing them simply means asking them.

Realism=pessimism

It's time to take reality back from the bottom-line crowd. When they say 'be realistic' they mean 'assume the worst, be pessimistic'. If someone has underestimated sales potential, no one calls out the ultimate putdown: 'Be realistic.'

The Web itself was not a realistic proposition: the world's largest network created without management or control? The Web is as implausible as a bumblebee flying. Both are flat impossibilities.

Businesses that define 'realism' as 'pessimism' will miss all the interesting opportunities.

Personal work time

The decentralisation of time creates other ripples. When you allow people to control their own schedules, they don't always cut their day into clean work and nonwork time periods. Their personal lives begin to invade Fort Business. They know that even if they leave for an hour for the Good News Assembly at their child's elementary school, they still can get done what needs doing, even if it means working at home over the weekend.

Once the time wall is breached, it rapidly becomes more and more permeable. If the only time I can make calls to further the process of adopting a child is during work hours, I will make those calls. If the only time I can talk with a travel agent to plan my vacation is between nine and five, I will call the travel agent during work. And, of course, the Web makes it easier than ever for me to permeate my work time with personal errands and concerns.

Now, the fact is that office workers have always ignored the temporal walls and called the adoption agency and the travel agency during work hours. We've just had to lie and pretend: Sorry to have a life, sir. It won't happen again, sir.

Some businesses have started to recognise that the temporal walls are full of windows. For example, Aetna realised that their workers inevitably spend time at work on personal issues. And what sort of fish-hearted bastard would tell them not to? So, Aetna built into its intranet the sort of information they thought employees were looking for. You can get information about how to adopt a child, for example, or how to arrange for a college scholarship for your kids. Since people are going to spend 'business time' doing that anyway, why not make it easier for them by including the information on the corporate intranet?

Yes, doing this had a practical purpose that speaks to the bottom-line guys because it meant employees were spending less time on nonbusiness issues. But you don't need bottom-line reasons to do this type of thing if we take as a basic business principle that companies need to wake up and smell the coffee. The walls around Fort Business may have inscribed in them, 'Let all who enter here abandon all personal life', but only the truly pathetic pay it any mind. Therefore, you might as well drop the pretence.

Skimming time

Let's review, shall we? The Web's decentralisation of time breaks apart the master schedule that supposedly has us ticking and tocking in unison, using artificial deadlines to enforce the corporate will. And personal time infects the purity of our time working behind the Fort walls.

One more thing: the Web changes time from sequential to random.

If you already know what 'random access' is, feel free to jump over this paragraph (but not before snickering at its witty self-reference). For example, audio is a sequential medium because you can only get from point A to point C by causing point B to pass the tape heads. CDs, DVDs, and hard drives are random access devices because you can hop all around on them.

The Web is (generally) random; you're expected to hyperlink around, sampling what you like. Random access spoils you. Instead of having to wait around for the tape to play out, you can skip right to the parts that you care about. (That also means each person's experience of the tape may be different.)

The Web is making us impatient with anything we can't *skim*. This includes:

- Sixty-seven-slide PowerPoint presentations
- Almost all meetings
- Being put on hold when you place a call that an adequate Web site would have made unnecessary
- Canned online tutorials
- Managers who hand you a copy of a report and then insist on telling you everything that's in it
- Television without a remote
- Travelling
- Bores

The point? Web time isn't just seven times faster than normal time. It's also a thousand times more random – in the good sense.

Open access to everything

When it comes to information, the Web's impulse is the opposite of Fort Business's. The Fort views information access as a publishing process, pushing to the appropriate people precisely the information they need at the right time. The publisher will ascertain your information needs. Your job is to sit back, relax and open wide.

This model made sense when information was scarce. And it made sense when business could take itself seriously as an omniscient potentate.

That was then. Now employees want to be able to run barefoot through the tall grass of information. And not simply because we're in a self-reliant sort of mood.

It's one thing to ask an information retrieval specialist to look up some data in a sanctified database where all the data is assumed to be approved and certified. It's another to try to gather competitive information from the Web where you're reading corporate BS from competitors, whining complaints on Usenet, reports from self-proclaimed industry experts (like, um, some of us Cluetrain authors), and libellous comments from anonymous stock manipulators.

In this environment, making judgments about what counts is a honed skill, one as personal as writing well or having a sense of humour. It is not something we're willing to delegate to others.

Ah, but the Central Committee says that it must control all access because it can't afford to let out state secrets. Imagine if our competitors got their hands on that stuff!

Sure, there are some trade secrets so important that you need to transport them in briefcases chained to some treasured bodily appendage: Coke's secret formula, a new molecule developed by a bioengineering company, the stocks a mutual fund company is about to invest in. But those are the exceptions. To talk about the role of secrecy in terms of those types of secrets is like evaluating the rural lifestyle by taking Ted Kaczynski's cabin as your example.

And there's a price to assuming that secrecy is normal, that everything is to be kept secret unless otherwise noted. Not only do you have the expense of keeping the secret, but you lose the value of information. Information by its nature only has value insofar as it's known. And, when combined with smart people with an impulse to solve problems and exploit opportunities, information increases its value.

Information wants to be free, sure. But it wants to be free because it wants to find other ideas, copulate and spawn whole broods of new ideas.

Controlling information is like trying to control a conversation: it can't be done and still be genuine. You're not publishing information, you're building a kitchen, you're planting a field. People wander around in information and learn where to find the stuff that counts, the stuff that's wrong in enlightening ways, the stuff that's purposefully off-base, the stuff that's fun, the stuff that's ludicrous.

Let's look at one specific type of information that needs to be free: documents.

Heroic documents

Business currently has a heroic view of documents. When we're given an assignment – 'Should we do this merger?' 'We need a plan for moving into the new office space' – we go to our desks and put our heads down for a day, a week, a fortnight. We go through as many drafts as we have to until we have a killer document – a report or an overhead presentation, typically – that nails it all down, comes to conclusions, and is irrefutable.

> ### The CIA and secrets
>
> Maybe ten years ago, I heard a tale about the CIA. The agency went on a declassification rampage. It seems that – because the rules of declassification had been so broadly delimited, and the penalties for noncompliance were terrifying – nearly everything for the previous several decades had been classified top secret.
>
> Therefore the agency didn't know what was really top secret any more. Phone numbers to order-in pizza were filed along with the number of the Kremlin hotline.
>
> Because of fear, the categorisation of the information had become practically worthless.
> – Christopher Locke

Then we go to the big meeting and slap it down like Beowulf slaying Grendl. 'Here I stand,' we declare, bravado masking our anxiety. And if someone calls our bluff, if someone says, 'Hmm, you seem not to have consulted the study the Gartner Group did last quarter' or 'You haven't considered the impact of the dilution of their shares,' you simply are not permitted to say, 'Whoops, heh heh, can I just have those copies back?' You're toast; you're dead meat; you've had your head handed to you.

What's gone wrong here is time. Because we are geared towards heroic presentations, we keep our work under wraps until we go public with it (that is, publish it) at the big meeting. Until that moment, no one is allowed to look at it without our permission. It is secret.

But the Web is changing this. There's already software that lets groups work together on documents over intranets. And that capability is being built into the word processors themselves so that it'll be as easy to post a draft to a shared Web space as it is to send it to be sprayed on paper.

So, you'll be given an assignment and, just as before, you'll retire to your cubicle, but only for about half an hour. You'll write up some initial ideas, post them to the intranet – this feels like saving them into a shared folder – and you'll send out mail to the people you think can help you with this. (Here's how much attention you'll pay to where these people are located in the organisation chart: zero.) Your e-mail will say, and I quote:

> **Old Man Withers wants me to solve the Parchesi problem in Tahiti. By next month! Yikes! So, I posted a couple of ideas at https://rsmythe.megacocorp.com/parchesi. I also put in some links to Donkeyballs' (oops, I mean Donnerby's) bogus report from last year, the one that didn't see the crisis coming. You can always count on Donkeyballs. ;-) There are also some links to a couple of sites I found when I did a search at the usual-suspect search sites.**
>
> **Let me know what you think. And remember, the doc I posted is just a bunch of BS. Kick it around, and let's get this thing going ...**
>
> **Thx, guys and gals. You's the greatest!**

This may not sound revolutionary, but consider:

- People used to keep their drafts secret for fear of looking like idiots, but now they post them and acknowledge they may be completely wrong.
- Work has gone from an individual task to a group task.
- The old model of keeping drafts secret until the moment of publication has been broken; ideas are now public from their inception.
- Ideas are assumed to be given out freely rather than hoarded.
- People are brought in not because they are in a chain of command but because they have necessary skills, share interests and are fun to work with.
- Sober-sided reports that were the mark of professionalism are often replaced by humour-filled interchanges.

Where do secrets fit into this picture? Fear of letting information out would cripple this project; the report that would emerge would be far inferior to what arises from a free interchange of ideas.

Besides, the Web lets everyone talk to everyone, in every department, across divisions, with strategic customers and even competitors. There are no secrets.

Decisions, decisions

Of course, you're not providing open access simply to fill people's heads with scurrilous thoughts and titillating tidbits. You want people to make better decisions. But open access to information also means that you've undercut your normal decision-making process.

Why do we have a decision chain in the first place? Ostensibly, it's because those up the organisation chart have a wider view as well as more experience. There is something to be said for experience, although it can thicken the skin as well as ennoble the mind. But if everyone has access to information, those on top no longer necessarily have the widest view. Being close to the customer and being in constant interaction with one's suppliers may bring an equally deep view into the business and its real possibilities.

Decisions are centralised also to enable accountability: praise for success, condemnation for failure. But every team member recognises – and often resents – this fiction. I sat through an off-site meeting once at which the middle managers were handed Cross pens to reward them for their success (but really to buy loyalty to the man handing them out). Afterwards one of the managers told me he felt dirty. Though his team had done the work, he got the pen. The pen was now a symbol of what he hated about his job. He would pass along the praise, of course, but clearly – he thought – senior management didn't appreciate how hard the team had worked. Being appreciated is not a commutative property – it requires eye contact, not the ritualistic passing of pens. And, of course, if the teams had failed, the senior executive accountable for the failure would have passed the criticism down and, not to be cynical, would likely find a way to dodge the bullet.

Does this mean that every decision will be collaborative? Of course not. But neither will every decision be taken by an individual.

We have a rich heritage on which to draw. Our culture has evolved many ways of making decisions simply because we have many ways of being together socially. For example, we seem to think having everyone vote works when it comes to running a country that can start wars, appropriate property and execute malefactors, yet we assume it's a bad way to run a business. There are lots of reasons for governance through voting, including ensuring that people have a say in setting policies that affect them, but one is particularly relevant to business: wisdom is a property of groups. In most instances, groups are collectively smarter than their individual members and often make more sensible decisions. The fact that typically the only group in a corporation that gets to vote is the board of directors is not an accident; decision making is usually more an exercise of power than an act of wisdom.

Of course, majority vote isn't the only way to make decisions. There's consensus, compromises, negotiations of every stripe, even counting eeny meeny. Yet for all this richness, in business we default to autocratic rulings. It seems a shame.

So, two outcomes are likely as the work of business increasingly moves online. First, we'll see more ways of deciding because we're seeing more ways of associating. Second, an important part of every project will be how you are going to decide.

Yes, this requires focusing on something we've often taken for granted before. But it will also open up for explicit discussion the nature of the social interaction in any particular project: is this a group effort, a team with leaders, a mob action, a ventriloquist act or some other type of human association? Even raising this for conversation in a group changes the dynamics, for it acknowledges the fact that there are lots of ways humans can work together – and every type of association is a matter of choice.

Unmanaging rich data

All this open information sounds like a nightmare to most of us. But in fact, *information* is the wrong term for it; we just don't have anything better.

The term *information*, as we commonly use it today, is a product of the computer age. Before then, *information* meant something like *news*. The term took on special meaning first in information theory, where it received a mathematical definition (to the yawning indifference of the awaiting public) and then in the computer world when *data* was invented.

As everyone who's taken Computer Science 101 knows, information consists of significant correlations of data. 'Ants #1–#100 died at 8:58' is data. 'Ants #1–#100 ate mayonnaise from the office cafeteria at 8:51 and died at 8:58' is information.

Row and column view of the world

Last_Name	First_Name	Start_Date	Employ_Level	SSN
Aardvar	Hyman	03-13-1992	J4	012-34-5678
Antear	Marjo	11-07-1998	B3	876-54-3210

'Information' is the stuff that goes into computers. And we all understand that to get the relevant facts about the world into our databases, we have to strip out a lot of the subtleties. For example, when we're populating our employee database, we have fields for 'Name', 'Start_Date' and 'Salary', and maybe one for 'Hobbies', but we certainly don't have fields for 'Hates_Thai_Food', 'Can't_Remember_Names', 'Hums_While_Reading' and the things we know about our co-workers that together constitute a context for working with them.

We strip out the context because that enables us to manage information: we select rows based on the content of the columns, we sort and arrange the rows, we look for interesting correlations of rows and columns. In short, information is stuff we generate precisely to be managed with computers.

The Web isn't about information, however. While it takes a database administrator or data entry specialist to enter data into a database, it takes any idiot with a computer to post something – from naked pictures of your cat to an overheated manifesto – on an intranet or on the Web. And it's only going to get easier.

So, while we're populating our corporate databases with context-less, stripped-down information that can be managed, we're populating our new Web world with every type of artefact the human hand can devise without a thought about how it will be managed.

Information is built to be managed; the stuff on the Web is the product of the lack of management. Information is stripped down; the content of the Web is rich in its contextuality. These two sets of contrasts go together.

Rich content and human voice

The stuff on the Web tends to be rich, not dry disquisitions loaded with charts and tables. Rather than a nicely printed report entitled, 'An Analysis of Competitive Strengths and Weaknesses of Product #456-A', you're more likely to get 'Why "Gosh Honey You Smell Great for a Corpse"™ Sucks but Will Rule the Underworld Anyway'.

There are bunches of reasons why this is so.

The Web is a document world. Eons ago, there was the Internet and it was populated by a subculture of Jolt-drinkin', four-eyed, research-crazed academigeeks who used a Unixlike language to ferret out morsels of information. (Unix is the Klingon of cyberspace – an argot only the true fanatics learn.) Along came the Web with two simple additions to the Internet.

First, the Web replaced screens and terminal emulations with a much more familiar and useful way of presenting stuff to be read: documents.

Second, the Web made it easy to hyperlink to a document without requiring the author's consent. This made it possible to navigate the Web by clicking on content rather than by typing in path names.

The Web succeeded where the Internet failed, in other words, simply by adding a document front-end and hyperlinking those documents together. The document user interface made it simple for people to get started with the Web. (Here's the instruction manual for a Web browser: if it's blue and underlined, click on it.)

This is important because documents are our most richly evolved type of data. Our culture has spent a couple of thousand years figuring out how to express virtually any type of thought on pages. Because we are so close to documents in all their forms, it can be hard to realise just how good we are at reading them and just how much contextual information they convey. We parse the structures of a page instantly and thus can tell the footer from the footnotes, the header from the headlines, the byline from the lines of bile. Computers still can't match us at this; just ask any user of optical character recognition software.

> ## The power table
>
> Suppose you removed the table from your conference room and replaced the seats with armchairs. Suppose you turned it into a living room. How much would this affect your meetings? That's how much your meetings are about power, not communication.

The Web is a document-based medium. It is built to handle the richness of documents. And, interestingly, the very first improvements of HTML (the language in which Web pages are written) mainly concerned themselves with simply enabling Web pages to look more like spiffy *printed* pages.

So, we're used to documents, documents are capable of handling a huge range of human expression and ways of structuring ideas, and the Web lets us maintain this sophisticated way of communicating.

The world of information on the Web is, therefore, a whole lot richer than the domain of database information in both content and structure.

But, wait, there's more!

The Web is a voiced world. The Web is the realm of the human voice. As we discussed in Chapter 2, your voice isn't simply the sounds that come out of your mouth. It's the way you present yourself in public through speech, writing, dress, body language, manners – virtually all that you do. The Web liberates voice by making it so damn easy to communicate and publish.

We have been trained throughout our business careers to suppress our individual voice and to sound like a 'professional', that is, to sound like everyone else. This professional voice is distinctive. And weird. Taken out of context, it is as mannered as the ritualistic dialogue of the 17th-century French court.

We may be accustomed to the professional voice, but it isn't natural, God-given or neutral: it's the voice of middle-aged white men who will do anything to keep people from seeing how frightened they are.

If you need to hear how the professional voice sounds, dig out any memo you wrote four years ago and compare it to how you'd write an e-mail about it now. A professional memo obeys implicit rules such as one page is best, no jokes, admit no weakness, spellcheck it carefully and send it to as few people as possible.

Now, we write e-mails. They're short, pithy, funny, they sound like us and we cc the CEO on a whim. That's why most of us don't want to use a word processor to write our e-mails. We want to be free of the expectation that we've spellchecked it or even re-read it before firing it off. We certainly don't want to waste our time monkeying with fonts and margins. At most, we'd like to be able to make words bold by hitting the keys harder.

E-mail enables us to construct our voices at our leisure, resulting in some odd artifices. A voice is, after all, a complex 'thing'. We have different voices for different environments and even for different people – we don't talk to our co-workers precisely the same way we speak to our children (well, unless we are very senior managers). Because most of our communications over the Web are 'asynchronous' – i.e., not real time back-and-forth – we can construct our presence a bit more carefully. Our culture is currently in a phase where people are trying on voices, discovering what works and what doesn't work over e-mail, bumping up against the limits, and making lots of mistakes. For example, while e-mail can replace many meetings (primarily because at a physical meeting you can't skim over the remarks of dunderheads), e-mail is a profoundly bad medium for conveying personal criticism precisely because it is textual and thus not very *con*-textual.

Here's another way the voice of e-mail is destroying committee meetings: after the carefully controlled meeting is over and the bigwigs are congratulating themselves on how well they managed it ('I think we got exactly what we needed out of that meeting, JB'), the 'junior' people are back in their cubes firing off e-mails parodying the results and pillorying the personalities. Meeting go boom.

The return of voice is dooming not only the memo and the pointless, drone-a-thon meeting, it's also turning the corporate propaganda newsletter into a flat-out embarrassment. Instead, individual 'zines are popping up in organisations, written by people with points of view, human voices and usually a sense of humour. For example, at Optika, a small software company in Colorado Springs, Sean Spradling, a 26-year-old member of the Marketing department, just up and began publishing *Forecast This*!, an internal 'zine that presents Sean's highly biased view of the market and Optika's marketing efforts. If 'uplifting' characterises most corporate newsletters, 'skewering' characterises *Forecast This*! But its readers – the salesforce, marketing and most of Optika – know to trust it, and look forward to getting it because it's written in a real voice stating the real truth. What a concept.

> **E-mail expectations**
>
> When you receive an e-mail you expect it to be:
>
> - Brief
> - Funny
> - Hastily written
> - Ill-considered
> - Thoughtless
> - Regrettable
>
> **All part of the charm!**
> – Christopher Locke

In a hyperlinked organisation, voice plays the old role of the organisation chart, telling you whom you should work with. That Mary is the Under-VP of Expectation Deflations for the western semi-region tells you nothing. That Mary is wicked smart, totally frank and a trip to work with tells you everything.

Thus do the formal bonds dissolve, replaced by the sound of the human spirit.

Telling stories

The world is more like a huge set of messy hyperlinks than like a really big table of data. It is a world in which information isn't abstracted into some seemingly neutral means of expression but is always uttered by some particular human in that person's own voice.

The knowledge management impulse

Knowledge management has become a hot topic precisely because we silently recognise that our information isn't yielding understanding. But information is unsatisfying precisely because it's managed; to make it manageable, we strip out context and voice. So, if we identify something called knowledge and then insist on managing it, we'll repeat the problem that gave rise to our desire for knowledge.

Conclusion? If you want to get past information, you have to give up the hope of managing your – and others' – understanding of the world. Also, you can't do it yourself: all understanding is social, by definition.

So what happens to information management?

On the one hand, it continues much as it is. We still need databases that reduce people to numbers. Couldn't live without 'em. But we also should recognise that the increase in available information has made us feel stupider than ever. All the printouts, all the database dumps and all the nicely formatted reports and spreadsheets with embedded charts are not describing our world to us. It's just not adding up. We have statistics but no understanding. And adding more and more information is only increasing the noise level.

We don't need more information. We don't need better information. We don't need automatically filtered and summarised information. We need understanding. We desperately want to understand what's going on in our business, in our markets. And understanding is not more or higher information.

If you want understanding, you have to re-enter the human world of stories. If you don't have a story, you don't have understanding. From the first accidental wiener roast on a prehistoric savanna, we've understood things by telling stories. I don't mean fiction or stories heavy with plot; I mean narratives that string events together in time and show them unfolding.

For example, my young son in some sense understands World War II. His story is this: the Nazis attacked other countries and were winning until the USA stepped in and beat the Nazis.

A Russian child's story about World War II is likely to be very different: The Allies delayed opening a second front until the incredible sacrifices Russia made wore the Nazis down, and then the United States finally came in and finished the job.

Both stories are ways of understanding the war.

My son doesn't understand the First World War because he doesn't have a similar sort of story, right or wrong. ('Once upon a time, there was an archduke …')

Here's another example. I worked at a company that failed for lots of good reasons. When a bunch of us ex-employees get together, some of us say that it was because the product got too inbred and complex; others say that Marketing failed to predict the platforms the software would have to run on; others say that the management team was too focused on new products and ignored the bread and butter. None of us tells the same story. And that means that we, as a group, don't understand what happened.

That's a sign of trouble, as we point out in the previous chapter. The company's origins are part of its authentic identity. That identity gets expressed in stories that sound something like these:

- Our founders were living in a garage and came up with an idea for 'mistake management'. They thought it'd be great for law offices, but it turned out that lawyers are late adopters of technology. Then, at one of the law firms they called on, they noticed that the secretaries were mixing Wite-Out with cream soda because …

- We're 157 years old, and started out making faux papyrus, which was in great demand during the great Egyptian interior decorating craze in the mid-1850s. When that died out, we realised that we had manufacturing equipment that – if you just adjusted the thickness – could just as easily turn out prefab walls. And that headed us in the direction we're still in …

- This company was founded by tech weenies and got off a great product real early in the 3D fax market. That was a time when being first mattered more than anything, and the company lived on peanut butter and cheap drugs. But, you know how it is, you hit a wall where you have to bring in the suits. So, we went out and hired the former COO of Sears ...

When you get past the mission statement and the slide showing why your current market share and revenues are making Croesus envious, and you start to tell your story, only then do people begin to understand your company.

And it's not just companies that have stories. Every sale worth knowing about has one ('It looked like the bad guys were going to win this one, so I wrote this e-mail, see, and sent it to this guy I know ...'). Every repair job has one ('I tried everything in the book to get the X405 to work, including repacking the bearings, which is a total pain. And then while I was tightening the booster ring, I noticed the damndest thing ...'). Every product has one ('We couldn't figure out why no one was using the cup holders in the Deluxe model, so we did a study and we discovered that the engine is so powerful that people were afraid to let go of the wheel. So we decreased it from 36 to 12 cylinders and scored a hit with the scaredy-cat driver market ...').

We live in stories. We breathe stories. Most of our best conversations are about stories. Stories are a big step sidewise and up from information:

- Unlike information, they have a start and a finish.
  The order counts a lot.

- They talk about events, not conditions.

- They imply a deep relationship among the events, a relationship characterised overall as 'unfolding' as if the end were present in the beginning – as of course it almost always is (as was foretold, in a fractally recursive sense, by Aristotle at our culture's beginning).

- Stories are about particular humans; no substitutions allowed.

- Unlike a set of economic forecasts or trends analysis, they do not pretend to offer the certainty that life will continue to work this way. (On the other hand, the story is more likely to be correct than the forecast because it takes all of our current understanding of the world to accept a story.)

- Stories are told in a human voice. It matters who's telling it.

So, stories are not a lot like information. But they are the way we understand.

How to apply this to your workaday world? You already have. When you are telling someone how you won this account or lost that one, when you are explaining why the competitor's trade-show booth was a disaster, or when you are telling a financial analyst how the market got to be as wacky as it is, you're already telling stories. You can't help it. You're human. Stories are how we make sense of things.

Anything else is just information.

Brokenness

Stories are a way to understand a world that can surprise us. But in Fort Business, surprises are a sign of the failure of management. Management aims at predictability and it tries to get there via control.

The urge to manage is deep in our culture. It ultimately is defeated by the fact of human fallibility.

It's in the Web's nature to 'always be a little bit broken' because it's decentralised. No one is in charge of making sure that the page you're trying to get to hasn't been taken down. There's no one to fix the Web, no one to plan it, and no one to complain to.

Seven ways to tell stories

1. Ban the opening joke. Begin your next PowerPoint presentation by saying, 'Let me tell you a story ...' and then recount what made the market the way it is, what got your company to come up with such an incredible product, and what obstacles particular customers faced and overcame by using your product.

2. Make sure the forms you use to 'collect knowledge' have big empty boxes in them so the story can be told.

3. Every meeting with a potential partner, every exciting sales meeting, every important encounter with customers can best be told as a story. Do so.

4. Turn your next white paper into a narrative.

5. Collect the stories of your business and publish them on an intranet site.

6. Reward the tellers of good stories. They're the people everyone's listening to anyway.

7. Rewrite your mission statement as a corporate story. In fact, wouldn't a narrative version of an annual report help the company more than the usual hearty prose and canned snaps of happy employees?

In fact, all big systems are broken. We don't always see that because what counts as broken is a matter of perspective. For example, on the phone system sometimes we get busy signals, and sometimes the phone rings and rings and no one answers, but we choose not to count those as signs of brokenness. If the telephone system chose to treat busy and unanswered phones as broken, it could make answering machines a standard telephone service. We could even complain that we have to memorise long strings of numbers, instead of having cute phone 'numbers' like **david.weinberger.the.balding.one@brookline.ma.usa**.

We choose to see the phone system as basically not broken, and choose to see the Web as inevitably broken. Why? Because fallibility is an endearing trait that seems to be a requirement for community. We of course want the people we work with to do everything they can to meet their commitments to us, but we also may find it hard to trust people who refuse to admit fallibility – their own and others'. We are intensely uncomfortable with people who have no weaknesses. For example: Michael Jordan, Jesus and my older cousin Don.

The Web's frailty makes it more human, less threatening. It also lets us move faster. For example, Mark Gransee, VP of Information Systems at Eddie Bauer, said (in an article in *InformationWeek*):

> In the old cycle, you could … hit analysis paralysis. Now you can't be afraid
> to make a decision just because the conditions are going to change and make
> that decision obsolete.

He adds that perfectionism isn't allowed: 'You just have to do the best you can.'

Meanwhile, at Owens Corning, Mike Radcliff, CIO, said (also in *InformationWeek*):

> Our staff has to be able to work with incredible ambiguity, be
> self-confident, simplify and trust others … Most of all we have to embrace
> 'good enough' reengineering, good enough that we can progress … not
> necessarily what we'd do in the ideal world.

But it's not just systems that are imperfect. More important, so are we humans. Say it with me: humans are imperfect. I am imperfect.

Feels good, doesn't it?

We often use the phrase 'knowledge is power' to make it seem that hierarchically granted power is justifiable. In most hierarchies, however, knowledge isn't power, it's a weapon. Being right advances you and being wrong is a defeat. That sucks.

You can see the politics of 'being right' throughout most organisations. People win arguments – and thus secure their position in the hierarchy – through the cutting remark, through megatonnage of evidence, through agreeing with industry consultants, and through the smug refusal to ever admit being wrong.

> ### Cluetrain's own politics of rightness
>
> Cluetrain itself is prey to one particular Being Right stratagem: everything you know is wrong (in the words of Firesign Theater). Thus, our first temptation is always to find the way in which current beliefs are mistaken, preferably in some very clever and deep way.
>
> Knowing this, however, has not helped us get past it. Many more years of therapy are called for.

But wrongness has a lot going for it beyond the fact that some things can only be learned through trial and error. For example:

- Some people are great at generating ideas but terrible at thinking through their impact. You want them to have as many bad ideas as possible because they will thereby randomly generate more good ideas. (I tell my clients that I try to maintain a 9:1 ratio of bad ideas to good. And, no, I can't tell which are which. If only.)

- Errors are how assumptions become visible. And there is nothing more valuable than a newly discovered assumption, because only then can you see what's holding you back and what could propel you forward.

- There's too much to know, so all important decisions are, to some extent, random. By being free to make errors, you can try more paths until you stumble on one that takes you somewhere interesting (albeit probably not where you at first thought – mistakenly – you should be heading).

- Errors remind us that we're fallible humans. A company that's too embarrassed to admit mistakes and that builds a culture where being wrong is humiliating literally is denying what it is to be human. And you will pay the price – in this world, if not in the next.

- Mistakes give us something to talk about.

- Being wrong is a lot funnier than being right. The right type of laughter – laughter at what the mistake reveals about our situation rather than laughter aimed at a person who dares to be human – is enormously liberating. In fact, laughter is the sound that knowledge makes when it's born.

Does your company have 'zero tolerance' for error? Can you change your mind without losing status? If so, consider engaging in the radical politics of wrongness. Go out and commit a whopper. Then embrace it publicly.

It's a good feeling. It's liberating. It's how you find your voice.

Blurry boundaries

Webs have blurry boundaries. Fort Business, on the other hand, makes an enormous investment in maintaining the integrity of the walls.

Hyperlinked organisations never met a wall they liked.

In the world of closed rooms and weekly meetings, you're a member or not. To join, you have to commit to sitting in a room at a particular time. In the open, hyperlinked world, it requires nothing but a few clicks to check out what a particular group is doing. You join their e-mail discussion group or visit their group intranet site. Zero commitment. So membership isn't a yes-or-no decision. You can browse with all the lack of commitment the word implies.

When the hurdles to membership lower, the boundaries blur. The blurring isn't occurring only inside of the Fort. Businesses are building extranets to enable their strategic partners to access information. There are hundreds of examples of this, in industries that range from retailing to drilling for oil to distributing T-shirts to the people who print slogans on them.

In many cases, extranets are used to get the paper out of the system. This enables process automation and cost savings, which are good things. But some companies – and someday, all companies – are going farther than that, giving their partners and customers access to their own intranet, so they can see the sausage being made.

Intranet technology is sophisticated enough to let you control exactly who has access to what, so it's no longer an all-or-nothing proposition. You can let customers see product-design discussions but keep them from seeing what its competitors are saying to you; you can let a supplier check the processing of a payment but keep it out of the pages where your accountants are evaluating bids. You have all the flexibility you need. The old excuses for pulling up the drawbridge and keeping everyone out entirely just don't hold.

Why not let your customers see your product-design process? They know that it's not perfect. They know you're going to go down wrong paths, you're going to abandon pieces you thought were locked in, you're going to squabble senselessly over trivia. That's what business is like.

Every business is dysfunctional because everything human is at least a little bit broken. It's not an accident. It's the human condition.

So what are you protecting your customers from? The obvious truth they know and live with every day? Just exactly whom do we think we're fooling?

Companies that let their customers and suppliers into the process early on deliver better products. And they forge the bonds of trust and delight that are the only ones that work in the 'frictionless' Web.

But maybe you need more than the promise of riches. Perhaps you need the fear of failure to motivate you. So, here it comes: suppose you use your extranet solely as a secure publishing site or for automating transactions that otherwise require paper, rubber stamps and file folders. This will decrease your expenses and your time to market. Excellent. But if that's all you do, the first companies that knock down the walls to their customers and suppliers will eat your lunch and then beat up your children for their lunch money.

Imagine the Foobar Company, the leading supplier of pen chains to the banking industry. Its development process calls on it to come up with a marketing requirements document that results in a product spec that in turn results in a new product. The entire development process is done behind walls because Foobar can't let its competitor, Wumba Chains, find out what it's doing. But now Foobar has discovered that Wumba is letting its customers into Wumba's product-development processes way early in the game. As a result, Wumba's customers are ready with purchase orders the day the product ships, whereas Foobar's customers need months of explanations and wooing from the sales force. And while Wumba's customers feel they're getting the real poop, Foobar's customers find the carefully constructed and controlled press releases and product brochures to be barriers more than helpers. They have to sort through them to try to get a sense of what's real and what's wishful thinking.

So, Foobar decides to open the floodgates. Customers and suppliers are poking all around the innards of Foobar Company. These 'outside' companies are seeing the actual workings of the company, and that means they are getting to know the individuals in the organisation. They're learning that for questions about the safety features of pen chains, they should listen to what Paolo has to say, for information about retrofitting cars for advanced pen chains there's no better source in the industry than Mary, and when it comes to addressing future ideas for pen chains you should never, ever pay attention to what Amit says.

As this sort of knowledge gets absorbed, the 'outsiders' start dealing directly with the individuals and hyperlinked groups in the organisation. If a partner needs to know how the pen chains are going to work with the new government regulations, why go through Legal or Regulatory Compliance or Marketing which will take six months to formulate some ass-covering BS, when you can pop into a work site or have an e-mail discussion among the people who really know what's going on and will tell you the truth?

And when you pop into this group, are you going to know or care that in fact some of the members are in fact other partners of Foobar? If Juan is an articulate, knowledgeable, trustworthy voice in the discussion, will you know or care that he is in fact a supplier or an industry expert who works for one of Foobar's customers?

To the outside, the company begins to look like a set of hyperlinked clusters who select themselves based on trust and respect and even their sense of fun. The trust is built through the quality of voice of the participants: that is all that counts in a hyperlinked team.

The business now consists of a shifting set of hyperlinked groups, self-organising, inviting in participants based on the quality of their voice, regardless of where – and whether – they are on the organisation chart. Management is simply an impediment to these groups. In fact, rather than employees feeling that they must constantly justify themselves to management, management now needs to give workers a single reason why it should be involved in the life of the business it used to believe it ran.

Hyperlinks subvert hierarchy. Hyperlinks subvert Fort Business.

Business is a conversation.

The economy of voice

No one's asking you to decide if you want to run your business using the Web. It's a done deal. The Internet has already set expectations for how connections ought to work. The gulf is there; a gulf caused, ironically, by the abundance of connection.

The Web is the sum of these connections. It isn't a medium, a new type of intercom, or an invention like really cool wristwatch walkie talkies. It is a broad, open place that lets everyone touch everyone else and touch every digit of information by twitching a wrist and tapping a single finger.

What connects you to me to everyone else are Web pages and e-mail and chat and discussions. These are all artefacts of human voice. Each is deliberately created and put forward as our public self, the self that is closest to us and, paradoxically, least known to us.

An economy of voice. Has there been such a thing since the Athenians talked democracy into existence?

The voices are heard in conversations. That's why the Web has its transforming power: it turns out the fundamental elements of our world have been products of deep conversations all along – conversations carried on by philosophers, artists, poets and other crafters of language. Had those conversations across the generations been different, we would not have the world we do.

These particular conversations have given rise to a deterministic, causal world in which outputs result from inputs according to natural principles and self-evident rules. The world's mechanism depends not only on predictable – and thus interchangeable – parts but also on the centrality and predictability of laws of nature, principles of behaviour, and time itself, a recent achievement in our history. (Socrates never said, 'Hey, Alcibiades, what do you say we meet at the corner of Hesiod and Pericles at 3.15? Later, babe.')

Physical laws, rules of behaviour, contracts, schedules, deadlines, professionalism, organisation charts and management practices are all types of connections. They all are attempts to control not only the object of the connection but also the nature of the connection itself. Why? Because they promise control over the two things we fear most: the vicissitudes of our world and the passion of our selves. As a manager armed with a theory and the latest business book, I not only know what to do, I know who to be.

Then the Web crept into our offices under false pretenses. We thought first it was a library of information. Then we thought it was a publishing medium. Then we thought it was a toy or a dangerous distraction. But in fact it is a conversation of a new type, free of the need to get permission from Dad and his army buddies.

New types of connections. The heart flowing to other hearts. A new rhythm. A new causality. A new understanding of power. Conversation that understands that it isn't a distraction from work, it's the real work of business.

The Web is hitting business with the force of a whirlwind because it is a whirlwind. The closely held, tightly packed, beautifully tooled pieces are being pulled apart. They are rebinding themselves in patterns determined by the conversations that are occurring in every conceivable tone of voice.

The character of business is becoming the same as the character of the Web – an explosion reconfigured by the intersection of hearts.

CHAPTER [6]

E-Z answers

CHRISTOPHER LOCKE
and David Weinberger

Tell 'em what you told 'em

FROM THE FURTHEST REACHES of Jump Street, markets have been conversations. Craft and voice were joined at the hip – what you made was how you spoke. But then it turned out that the world was round, there were other places across that Big Blue Wet Thing, and trade routes got longer, natch. Producers became further removed from markets. Gradually, marketing became an abstract pipe down which producers shipped products to customers, though nobody would invent FedEx for several centuries. Somewhere along the line, speech and craft lost each other's phone numbers.

At the beginning of the Industrial Revolution, new power sources replaced much human grunt work. Producers immediately saw that this was a Good Thing. Moreover, they saw that repeatable processes and interchangeable parts were an Even Better Thing, as such mechanisation led to significant economies of scale – a fancy way of saying more money.

By the time the 20th century rolled around, industry hit upon an even more potent multiplier: interchangeable workers. The assembly line turned workers into machines. Through this stroke of genius, craft skill was effectively hosed, and workers were told to shut up and do what they were told.

Economies of scale also required economies of management. Telling them what to do efficiently required a new form of business organisation. Bureaucracy fine-tuned the division of labour needed to make this new setup work, and a breakthrough concept called the organisation chart determined who got to speak at all. Welcome to management by command and control. This resulted in *huge* economies of scale – a fancy way of saying 'robber barons.'

Mass production led to mass marketing, which led to (ta-da!) mass media. Broadcast applied the fundamental mass-production brainstorm to marketing communications. This development signalled the dawn of junk mail. Corporate speech became mass produced 'messages' jammed into a one-way spam cannon aimed at a dream that hasn't faded since: interchangeable consumers.

Ignoring the clear lessons of history (for example, the nuking of Hiroshima and the saturation bombing of Dresden), upstart 'foreign' companies started selling into markets the United States figured it had permanent dibs on. Guess again. The global economy threw a monkey wrench into the sweet deal that was mass production. Established markets broke up into a zillion micromarkets, leading to an explosion of new products and services: now you could get a car specifically designed for your urban, sports, just-divorced, hockey-fan lifestyle. Or whatever.

New knowledge was desperately needed to fuel this expansion, and this is when companies discovered what workers had long suspected but never talked about except in the washroom: management didn't know its ass from a hole in the ground. (See clear lessons of history, above.) While managers had got really good at bossing people around, they didn't know much about how things actually got made. This naturally resulted in many exciting high-level executive-type conferences about 'The Knowledge Deficit'.

Slowly (some are still attending summer school), companies began to realise that workers knew more than they'd been letting on – mostly because no one had asked them for about a hundred years. This led to the re-emergence of craft in the workplace, and a concomitant revaluing of speech – a fancy way of saying 'lead, follow or get out of the way'.

Ideas, talk and conversation were now encouraged among workers because they helped to deliver what organisations so desperately needed: a clue. During this period (which unfortunately ended in large measure due to 'downsizing' – but that's another story), 'empowerment' became the watchword of the day, and organisation charts were upended or tossed out altogether at companies like GE, Ford, Motorola, Corning, Cadillac and Federal Express (which by now, of course, had been invented). This was the era of the US Department of Commerce's Baldrige Award when the pursuit of Quality – always capitalised – took on a decidedly religious fervour. What Quality really meant was: 'We changed our minds. Please don't check your brain at the door.'

While speech was actively elicited from workers because it carried suddenly invaluable knowledge, it was not yet sought in any significant way from customers – a concept still perceived by many corporations as more dangerous than godless communism and universal healthcare combined. However, due to market fractionation, 'consumers' had already become far less interchangeable.

Then along came the Internet and all hell broke loose.

Just as the global economy had precipitated exponential growth in the array of choice among new products and services, so the Net caused an explosive proliferation of choice among new information sources. The broadcast model faltered and failed online. Embarrassing attempts to force it to work, such as 'push', were quickly swept under the rug – where, in the form of a large pig-in-the-python lump, they continue to trip up wannabe online businesses.

By its nature, Internet technology encourages open distributed speech, a fancy way of saying 'tellin' it like it is'. The human voice is the primary attractor, both *to* the medium and within it. Markets and workers are once again crafting their own conversations, and these conversations are also about craft – things we do that we actually care about.

As a result of the profound and unexpected changes wrought by the Net, the 200-year-long industrial interruption of the human conversation is finally coming to an

end, both inside companies and in the marketplace. That's what
www.cluetrain.com basically had to say when it hit the Web in 1999.

And you should see the flame-mail we got! This is because we're now living in a
period that could be called 'the Hangover'. Command and control is widely
perceived as dysfunctional, but it's a hard-to-break habit. Many business leaders are
well aware that bureaucratic hierarchy works against needed knowledge and
communication, yet inertia is a powerful force. ('The cluelessness is strong in this
one, Darth.')

Though the Internet represents an unprecedented invitation to break out of this
impasse, many organisations today resemble the Berlin Wall – monoliths interposing
themselves between the internal conversation of the workforce and the external
conversation of the marketplace. They are still pumping out mass-produced
messages, still trying to control workers and consumers, still trying to create mass
markets based on old industrial models.

Via intranets, workers are already speaking among themselves. Via the Internet,
markets are already speaking among themselves. The convergence of these two
conversations is not only necessary, but inevitable. Why? Because markets,
unencumbered by corporate bureaucracy and the need to ask permission at every
turn, are learning faster than organisations. Markets are therefore coming into a
new ascendancy, a fancy way of saying 'We rule, dude!' And increasingly, we value
only two qualities:

1. The engagement and passion-for-quality of genuine craft.
2. Conversations among recognisably human voices.

The simple, if painful, prognosis: organisations must encourage and engage in
genuine conversation with workers and markets – or go belly up.

So what, if anything, can businesses do at this juncture? They can begin by
searching out people within the organisation who understand what's going on. In
almost every case, they're there. Make friends with them. Make friends with the
marketplace again. Start listening. Find your voice. Then start talking as if your life
depended on it. It does.

Business is being transformed, but not by technology. The Web is simply liberating an atavistic human desire, the longing for connection through talk. That's the one constant throughout our evolution, from caves to mud huts to open-air bazaars, from city-states to empires, nations, interdependent global powers. We've always conversed, connecting to the people of our world in our authentic voices. We connect to ourselves the same way; that's the mystery of voice.

But part of us still has a deep resistance to the unmanageability of the Web. We keep wanting to contain it within a business model, to build it into our business plans and see it as an yet another 'opportunity' for more/cheaper/ faster/better business-as-usual. E-commerce, oh boy! *Ka-ching!* The sound of the cash register is all too often the sound of attempts to co-opt the Web. To tame it, domesticate it, make it more familiar. To shoot it, stuff it and mount it in the corporate board room along with the other trophies of corporate conquest.

At the same time that it spooks us, we're fascinated. We've been waiting for the Web to happen all along. We've been hating our jobs for generations. We've been longing to speak in our own voices since we made the Faustian deal to keep quiet in the first place. The Web is not aimed at business in particular. It wasn't built for business, it isn't fundamentally about business, and it can't be controlled by business – any more than the Internet could be controlled by the Pentagon that sponsored it.

The Web is inherently and intrinsically free. Businesses will perceive this fact as either a blessing or a curse depending on how much they value freedom, a quality of mind and heart not typically underscored in the average corporate mission statement.

Loaded questions

Literature is the question minus the answer.

Roland Barthes

If love is the answer, could you please rephrase the question.

Lily Tomlin

Overheard at the cocktail party that was the 1990s:

'So what's going to happen with all this Web stuff?'

'Where's it going? What are the trends? What are the directions?'

'Who's going to win?'

And they say there's no such thing as a dumb question.

Continents drifting across the oceans have trends. Bullets have directions. Cannonballs have trajectories. The future doesn't. The future is the intersection of choice and interruptions. The Web – what a surprise! – is more like the future than a cannonball. It will be what we make of it.

This leads to a funny conclusion. Ironic, actually. We ask questions about the future of the Web because we think there's a present direction that can be traced into the future. But in fact, the questions we ask aren't going to predict the future. They will create the future.

Not to get all heavy and ontological, but since questions are a type of conversation, it looks a bit like conversations give the world its shape, doesn't it? Questions do the spade work. They prepare the ground for answers. Be careful what you ask or you just might become it.

So far, the questions about the Web we hear the most – the ones some journalists use to stir up fear, the ones some politicians use to prepare us for the revelation that they just happen to be our saviours, the ones most businesses use to keep us in line and to sell us more stuff – these questions are actually decisions to look for the same old things. Their assumptions are wrong, and the answers they call for are mean-spirited. The questions themselves are intended to confuse the issue, and the answers are nothing but the smirk on the face of someone who just proved himself right.

There are other questions possible, better questions. Questions that come from the heart, not the wallet, the gonads or the lobe of the brain responsible for smugness. Questions that open the future instead of making sure the dead bolt on the door is nice and tight.

For example, take the ever-popular question, *Will the Web become a broadcast medium? Will it become TV?* That's vitally interesting to media titans who see the Web as a threat to how they make money. But that's not a question of the heart.

What the heart wants to know is, When the buttons at our fingers let us talk with the polyglot world's artists, how will we cope? What will we share as a culture and community? What will we talk about together? What will we laugh about? What type of laughter – mocking, ironic, cynical, sinister, belly-shaking guffaws – are we going to hear? Will we find we all share a common sense of humour, or will we learn to laugh in new languages? When will we record the first case of Web inebriation, a transglobal xenophilia induced by pure, uncut connectedness?

Here's a question beloved of industry analysts and others who think the point of conversation is to appear smart: *How quickly will commerce move to the Web?* Let's trot out the charts and studies, confident that at least one of them is going to turn out to be right.

But is this question really so important, or does it just address a detail about timing? Is your business going to be transformed if it turns out we're not going to hit the gazillion mark until 2004 instead of 2003?

But there is a heartfelt question lurking here. It has to do with the things of the world that quench our thirsts and raise our souls. It has to do with our fear of replacing the shops – and the neighbourhoods they enable – with a paper-souled efficiency that lets us search out and consume commodity products at disquietingly low prices. We're afraid that the last shred of human skin left on the bones of commerce is about to come off in our hands. We want to know how we'll reconnect to the other people in the market: buyers and sellers, people we know or whose faces are the landscape of our life in the agora. And we have this fear precisely because the e-commerce question has been asked wrongly so often, as if once commerce becomes virtual it will become cruelly automatic. We need to ask the heartfelt question about how we're going to talk about the things we care about, or e-commerce will indeed become nothing but the soundless scrape of coins over the wire.

Here's another question – top of the hit parade, actually – that steers us in a wrong direction as surely as asking, How can I drive straight to Hell, buddy? The question is, *What are we going to do about pornography on the Web?* This question seems to have nothing to do with business, but in fact it goes straight to the heart of maintaining a corporate wall between employees and customers, between internal and external behaviour.

The question has to do with drawing the line between the public and the private – no trivial matter since looking at the line is the quick and dirty way we decide who's civilised and who's savage, who's refined and who's a brute. The line between public and private is, of course, arbitrary, although we adamantly deny this by using every method of intimidation, from the law to dirty looks, to maintain it. The main point of the line is that there be a line – one that we can control.

And then we turn on our computer and filth comes pouring out of every orifice, from our e-mail inbox to our browser. Go to **whitehouse.com** and you discover it's a porn site. (Hint: next time, try **whitehouse.gov**.) Open an e-mail titled 'The info you asked about …' and get lewd invitations. Mistype a single letter of a Web address and you're staring at strange genitals in strange configurations. The Web isn't just redrawing the line, it's changing the nature of the line, making it explicitly permeable. But a new type of line means a new type of public.

So, our hearts ask questions, with dread as well as excited curiosity, about the new public world and its relation to the private. What is the relation of our night selves and our day selves, our self behind the company walls and outside of them? Why do we think of our private selves as our real selves? What would privacy be like if it weren't connected to shame? What is the fierce price we pay for every desire, every whim, every idea we stamp 'Secret'? To what degree are shame and embarrassment the expression of the will to control? If we abandon the illusion of controlling private behaviour, what type of public-ness will we have? How is the control we yearn to exert over the behaviour of others – at work and beyond – identical with the white-knuckle control we need to preserve our selves?

More questions meant to distract us: *How will we know what's junk on the Web and what's worth believing? How will we avoid being fooled by anyone with a plausible story and a Web address? What will be the new criteria, the new marks of authenticity?* These questions express a longing for someone to take charge of our knowledge. We want experts and authorities, just as we crave censors more than we crave sex and prefer certainty to freedom.

But our hearts have a different set of questions: when we can't rely on a central authority – the government, the newspaper, the experts in the witness box – for our information, what new ways of believing will we find? How will we be smart in a world where it's easier to look something up than to know it? How will we learn to listen to ideas in context, to information inextricably tied to the voice that's uttering it? How can we reverse our habit of understanding matters by jumping to further levels of abstraction and instead learn to dig into the concrete, the personal and the unique, told as stories worthy of our time?

We are – all of us – asked questions like, how will we manage (control) virtual workers in a distributed organisation?, when our hearts want to know how we are going to live with our families again.

We are asked, How are we going to keep our children safe on the Internet?, when our hearts also want to know what it would be like to be a child who can talk within the world's society of children.

We're asked, How can you tell if the person you're talking with is really the person you're talking with?, when our hearts want to know what people we will really become online and what having a disembodied identity will mean.

We are asked, How are the poor people of the world going to get Internet access?, when our hearts want to know how we can connect with the poor of the world, because there isn't a single person we don't want to talk with. And once we talk, we know the conversation will make palpable the injustice of today's economics.

Our job now is not to answer questions. It is to listen past the questions based on fear and to hear the questions of the heart. Why? Because the proper answer to a heartfelt question is a conversation, and conversations make the world.

Hit one outta the park

Good then. That ought to put all the wrongheaded questions to rest, right? No, of course not. Business-as-usual being what it is, the questions never quit. Companies have said yes, the Cluetrain ideas are interesting, but give us a place to start. A methodology. A suite of best practices maybe. A set of guidelines. For God's sake, something!

'What's the bottom line?' they want to know. 'How can my company profit from the coming transcultural train wreck? How can we leap tall buildings in Internet time, innovate faster than a speeding data packet, and establish Peace, Justice, and the American Way in hyperlinked global markets?'

Well ... OK. Because you've been so patient and read so bloody much, we'll let you in on the Secret of Our Success. Just follow the 12 easy steps below and you're sure to be on your way to fame and fortune in the exciting new world of Webusiness. (Caution: It is vital that you follow these steps precisely in the order given. Otherwise, we are not responsible for the mutant hellspawn you may inadvertently call forth from the realm of the undead.)

The Cluetrain hit-one-outta-the-park 12-step programme for internet business success

1. Relax
2. Have a sense of humour
3. Find your voice and use it
4. Tell the truth
5. Don't panic
6. Enjoy yourself
7. Be brave
8. Be curious
9. Play more

10. Dream always

11. Listen up

12. Rap on

Do these things and you just can't miss.

Of course, there's as much distance between this advice and the decisions you make every day as there is between 'Go forth and multiply' and '100 Ways to Pick Up Hot Chicks and Radical Dudes'. Still, we yearn for easy advice. It's so hard to give up the old wish for stimulus-response marketing and management. Hard to go back to the days of the 'talking cure' when psychotherapy meant years of slogging through memories and dreams instead of a slap on the back, and instructions to 'nurture the inner child' and eat two bran muffins every day. Hard to forget the televised version of Anna Karenina that goes from start to finish in two hours (the train comes to a screeching halt just in time) and reopen the musty volume and soak into every snow-flecked page.

Look, we'd love to derive 12 happy instructions from the wash of ideas swirling around us. Really. We could market those puppies like Tang in a sauna. Seminars, workbooks, T-shirts, coffee mugs …

But it doesn't work that way. This is an existential moment. It's characterised by uncertainty, the dissolving of the normal ways of settling uncertainties, the evaporation of the memory of what certainty was once like. In times like this, we all have an impulse to find something stable and cling to it, but then we'd miss the moment entirely. There isn't a list of things you can do to work the whirlwind. The desire to have such a list betrays the moment.

There may not be 12 or 5 or 20 things you can do, but there are 10 000. The trick is, you have to figure out what they are. They have to come from you. They have to be your words, your moves, your authentic voice.

The Web got built by people who chose to build it. The lesson is: don't wait for someone to show you how. Learn from your spontaneous mistakes, not from safe prescriptions and cautiously analysed procedures. Don't try to keep people from going wrong by repeating the mantra of how to get it right. Getting it right isn't enough any more. There's no invention in it. There's no voice.

Maybe we'd have more luck with the Cluetrain List of Don'ts than with a List of Dos. The first 94 items would be things like: don't snoop on your employees, don't build knowledge management systems and corporate portals that are nothing but funnels for the same old propaganda. Don't hire people who claim to be experts at increasing morale. And right at the bottom of the list, number 95, would be the most important one: don't rely on lists, self-styled 'gurus' or business books.

Scary, isn't it? Good. You ought to be scared. That's a realistic reaction. You want comfort? Invent your own. Exhilaration and joy are also in order. But face the facts: the tracks end at the edge of the jungle.

Post-apocalypso

CHRISTOPHER LOCKE

*We will strive to listen in new ways – to the voices of quiet
anguish, to voices that speak without words, the voices of
the heart, to the injured voices and the anxious voices,
and the voices that have despaired of being heard.*

Richard M. Nixon, first inaugural address, 1969

IRONY IS PERHAPS THE MOST COMMON mode of Internet
communications. The Net didn't create the mentality, but it did come along just in
time to give it new expression. Nixon speaking about unheard voices of the heart
from the height of the 1960s is a prime example of why most people have despaired
of ever being heard at all. And of why they've stopped listening for answers from
above – from Big Government, Big Business, Big Education, Big Media, Big Religion.
With few exceptions, the interlocking agendas of these monolithic powers have
become utterly divorced from the constituencies they were originally conceived to
serve, their interests as remote from our daily lives as the court of King George was
to the American colonies in 1776. And you know what happened then.

So are we calling for a revolution? What would be the point? The only revolution that matters is already well under way. And by the way, since it's not being covered by CNN and Fox, we're winning.

You say you didn't notice anything out of the ordinary? Nor were you supposed to. Invisibility and ignorance are powerful weapons.

Ignorance is not a value you often hear extolled. Let's make up for lost time. Here's how it works; it's pretty simple. When you ignore people long enough, they begin to feel invisible. Because your important concerns do not concern them, they begin to figure it's a two-way street. They begin to ignore you back. Pretty soon they're thinking Al Gore is some hockey player from Winnipeg and Warren Buffet … isn't he the guy who does late-night infomercials for cut-rate country western CDs? Three easy payments and it's yours? Yeah, but who really cares.

Ignorance is power. A maxim often heard online is that the Internet routes around obstacles, meaning it ignores them. In its early phase, the Net ignored business; Internet audiences simply weren't interested. And the feeling was mutual. Business ignored the Net for a long time, not seeing it as what it thought a media market should look like, which is to say television. This mutual ignorance served as the incubator for a global revolution that today threatens the foundations of business-as-usual.

Before any Old Order of Things can be given the final heave-ho coup de grâce, it's necessary to create a parallel infrastructure controlled by people acting in cooperation for their own benefit and mutual support. One thing any such effort requires is an extraordinarily efficient means of communication. We didn't used to have one. Telephones just didn't cut it.

Then, irony of ironies, along comes the Internet. It was as if we'd ordered it from Amazon: 'Hello, US Federal Government? Yes, we'd like one totally open, high-speed data backbone. Uh-huh, and charge that to the Department of Defence, why don't you? What's that? What do we want it for? Oh, just chatting about stuff. You know, this and that …'

Invisibility is freedom. At first it feels awful that no one can see you, that nobody's paying attention. Darn! But you get used to it. We've had 200 years to get used to it. Then one day you find yourself on a network, networking, and it dawns on you that it's like walking through walls. Wow! Like some comic-book-mystic Ninja warrior! That's pretty cool. You can get away with saying things you could never say if anyone took you seriously. Dilbert is just a comic strip. Hah-hah. Beavis and Butthead is just a cartoon. Heh-heh. And if anyone comes sniffing around and wonders if this Internet stuff could be maybe dangerous, culturally subversive, it's oh, hey, never mind us. We're just goofing off over here on the Web. No threat. Carry on. As you were.

But we aren't just goofing off. We're organising: building and extending the Net itself, crafting tools and communities, new ways of speaking, new ways of working, new ways of having fun. And all this is happening, has happened so far, without rules and laws, without managers and managed. It's self-organising. People by the millions are discovering how to negotiate, cooperate, collaborate – to create, to explore, to enjoy themselves.

But what's the point, asks business? Business always wants there to be a point, a goal, an objective, a plan. Otherwise, how would we manage?

There never was any grand plan on the Internet, and there isn't one today. The Net is just the Net. But it *has* provided an extraordinarily efficient means of communication to people so long ignored, so long invisible, that they're only now figuring out what to do with it. Funny thing: lawless, planless, management-free, they're figuring out what to do with the Internet much faster than government agencies, academic institutions, media conglomerates and Fortune-class corporations.

So what is the Net really good for? Besides chatting, that is. Well, there's the small matter of co-ordinating distribution. Remember those ancient markets from way back in the first chapter where we talked about trade routes and the cities that grew up where they intersected? Where caravans arrived with exotic merchandise and tried to sell their wares.

'Figs here! Delicious figs!'

'Give me one. Figs want to be free.'

'No way.'

'I won't buy from you if I can't have a taste. From where I'm standing, your figs smell like your camel pissed on them.'

'My camel is very well behaved. He never urinates.'

But enough about early advertising. One thing the Net is good for is organising markets. Especially if you're invisible and powerless, ignorant of how things are supposed to work, ignorant of business-as-usual. Especially if you're intent on end-running the empire.

Who has the stuff we like? Who makes the stuff we need? Interest, curiosity, craft and voice combine to create powerful self-organising marketplaces on the Web: 'Figs here, delicious figs!' Or it might be a faster chip, an elegant bit of code, a new idea, a joke, a line of poetry, a job. Stuff, as the digital world has taught us, isn't always stuff. And co-ordinating how it gets distributed is more like a cocktail party than a strategy session. Stuff gets around the way word gets around. Along the same routes. Around the same obstacles. Though motivated by altogether different principles than those driving business, this is not as chaotic as it may sound, nor as inefficient. It's happening right now, every day. It works. 'Follow the money' may still apply, but to find the money in the first place, follow the conversation.

In this book, we have tried to paint a picture of radical changes that are taking place today, aided and abetted by the Internet. But to people who've already lived in the Net for a while, these changes aren't perceived as radical at all. They're second nature. On the Web page we asked people to sign in support of the Cluetrain Manifesto, one comment was repeated over and over: *'It's about time!'*

We've talked about the ideas you've just been reading with hundreds and thousands of people online who don't ask for additional explanations. Yeah, they say simply, damn straight. These are people who 'get it', as the saying goes. They don't need explanations; they already know how it works.

'But ... but ... ' you may sputter, 'those are just disgruntled 'Net-heads' – I read all about them in *Time* or *TV Guide* or *Sports Illustrated* or somewhere. Those unemployable fringe types who never amount to anything anyway ...'

Don't bet on it. Here's a small handful of the radical organisations in which people who signed the manifesto work: Bank of America, Boeing, Cap Gemini, Cisco, Comcast, Compaq, Computer Sciences Corporation, Dow Jones, EDS, Ericsson, FedEx, Fleet Credit Card Services, Herman Miller, IBM, Intergraph, Kaiser Permanente, Kellogg, Kinko's, KPMG, Levi Strauss & Company, Lucent Technologies, Merck, Microsoft, Morgan Stanley Dean Witter, New York Life Insurance, Novell, Ogilvy Public Relations, Oracle, PeopleSoft, PricewaterhouseCoopers, Qualcomm, Saturn, Sears, Sema Group, Siemens, Sun Microsystems, US Interactive, the U.S. Internal Revenue Service, US West, USWeb/CKS, Wang, WR Hambrecht + Co., Ziff-Davis.

Stereotyping is a bitch, ain't it? Clichés are so comfortable and easy. Business is fat-cat moguls meeting in posh boardrooms atop steel-and-glass towers high above the jostling masses in the street. Stereotypes usually have some basis in reality, but they're lousy tools with which to frame critical judgments. More often than not, business happens in the streets, not above them. And so do revolutions.

But if you're looking for Molotov cocktails and tear gas, beleaguered cops and firebrand radicals, you're bound to miss what's really happening. Ruth Perkins of the Florida Department of Law Enforcement wrote to us, 'Thank you for solidifying the thoughts and mission I've had for so long. I'm a wholehearted signer and practitioner of your manifesto.'

Just because you're not seeing a revolution – or what Hollywood has told you a revolution ought to look like – doesn't mean there isn't one going down.

The demonic paradox

Although a system may cease to exist in the legal
sense or as a structure of power, its values (or anti-values),
its philosophy, its teachings remain in us. They rule our thinking,
our conduct, our attitude to others. The situation is a
demonic paradox: we have toppled the system but
we still carry its genes.

Ryszard Kapuscinski, Polish journalist, 1991

All talk of revolution notwithstanding, the struggle is already largely over. It's genuinely tough to find anyone who will stand up and defend the standard traditional conventional old-school way in which 'everyone knows' business should be conducted. As far as we can determine, not only does everyone *not* know it, nobody seems to believe it for a second.

This is odd, we think. And critically important to us, personally and professionally. After all, if we're hanging our asses out with this whole Cluetrain tirade, there had better be something there to carry on about. Right? Otherwise, wouldn't we look stupid?

So we rack our brains. We search our souls. We ask ourselves: are we making this stuff up? Is it wishful thinking? Are we maybe just having acid flashbacks? Ever uncertain of our findings, but always wishing to be scientifically precise, we're all constantly performing little sanity checks: 'Have I slipped the surly bonds of earth, or is it actually possible that nobody left alive today really believes this stuff any more?'

We meet a lot of people in our day-to-day work. A lot of different kinds of people – as random a sample as you could ever hope for. Unbeknown to them, they are being used as subjects – fodder if you will – for our ongoing market research. This involves looking for the perfect Suit, that is to say, the business person who fully embraces and embodies the corporate stereotype. So far, the closest we've come is some guy in a Dell TV ad: manly but understanding, firm yet gentle with his underlings. Always ready for a good laugh, but no joking around when it comes to delivering the goods.

What he really does is hard to tell, though it seems to have a lot to do with his Inspiron brand notebook computer. Man, he takes that baby everywhere!

But of course, he's a male model. So we're still looking. Most of the people we run across are rather disappointing in this respect:

'So how's the job going?'

'The job? How do you *think* the job's going? The job sucks.'

'Oh.'

Or maybe it's someone who just bought a new product online:

'Are you satisfied with your latest purchase?'

'What, are you yankin' my chain? Get away from me, you pervert.'

'Yes, sir. Sorry to have disturbed you.'

This is hard work. No lie. But we keep at it, relentlessly searching for the canonical business type or the ideal consumer. Neither seems to exist. Isn't that just too weird?

But here's something weirder still. If you take someone you've just been talking to in a normal, non-insane sort of way, and put him or her in trade-show booth, nine times out of ten this person will immediately start talking like a Suit: '… and we are very proud of our pre-eminent position with respect to our competitors. Dunderhead & Gladhand just ranked our company second in the entire industry and …'

… and it makes you want to go out and shoot yourself, or at least take a long hot shower. Then he or she comes offstage and says, 'So how did I do?'

You hem and haw. You want to be kind, but how to put it? 'That was total bullshit! How could you spout that patent crap? I know you don't believe a word of it.'

'Oh, that, of course not. But how did I do?'

Mr Kapuscinski, our Polish journalist from the quote above, says that although we may have toppled the system, we still carry its genes. He says it's a demonic paradox. Jazzman Rahsaan Roland Kirk has another term for this same phenomenon. He calls it *volunteer slavery*.

So while business stereotypes are largely empty, or come from another day and have long since lost any real descriptive power, we find ourselves replicating the behaviours they caricature. Why? Well, because we're business people, of course! And that's how business people behave. Welcome to the hall of mirrors. Welcome, as Vonnegut put it, to the monkey house.

We don't believe what we're saying at work. We know no one else believes it either. But we keep saying it because because because because the needle's stuck. The record's broken. Because we just can't stop. Because who would we be if we didn't talk like that?

Maybe we'd be free. Or freer at least.

In most cases, no one is forcing us to replicate these useless obsolete behaviours. We imagine we must, but we never investigate. We posit some organisational bogey man who'd punish us terribly if we were human. Give us a good hard whippin', you betcha.

What if there's nobody there, though? What if it's like Santa Claus, or flying saucers? Like Fox Mulder, we want to believe, we really do. Maybe it's like – uh-oh – God!

Not to be disrespectful, but there's a point here. Historically, capitalism depended heavily on the Calvinist notion that news of impending salvation was telegraphed by worldly success. Worker productivity positively skyrocketed under this inspired setup. It wasn't Santa who knew if you were naughty or nice, it was the Big Boss. So better knuckle down.

But, let's get real. A couple of centuries ago, a new invention arrived in the world. It was called 'the job'. The idea was simple, really. You went to some hellhole of a factory, worked 16 hours until you were ready to collapse, and you kept on doing that every day until you died. Cool, huh? You can see where Calvinism must have come in handy. Some people wouldn't do that even for stock options.

Among the many casualties of this arrangement was the human spirit. And of its necessary functions, conversation was the first to go. People would talk with each other while doing craft or cottage work. But talk interfered with factory production. And of course, there was Management. Management knew everything. Workers knew nothing. So shut up and get back to yer lathes and looms, ye dirty sods!

Fast-forward a hundred years or so and along comes 'knowledge work' – an even cooler invention that enabled us to have magazines like Fast Company and meant we were allowed to know something all of a sudden. Excuse us, management said, but would you mind letting us in on whatever it is, as we're rather tapped out over here?

And the rest, as they say, is history. A history that brings us right up to today with its rip-snortin' high-speed Internet with broadband everything, hold the mayo. Whoopee! But that's not the point. The point is what this latest technological wonder brings back into the world: the human story. A story that stretches back into our earliest prehistory. A story that's been in remission for 200 years of industrial 'progress'. When it breaks out again in the 21st century, it's gonna make Ebola look like chicken pox. Catch it if you can.

And next time you wonder what you're allowed to say at work, online, downtown at the public library, just say whatever the hell you feel like saying. Anyone asks you, tell 'em it's OK. Tell 'em you read about it in a book.

Put that in your demonic paradox and smoke it.

More about radishes

> *What do I know of man's destiny?*
> *I could tell you more about radishes.*

Samuel Beckett

So whaddya think? Will Cluetrain be the next Big Thing? Not if we can help it. Ditch the bumper stickers. Forget the catchy slogans and the funny hats. Let's not write the bylaws and pretend we did. Let's not start another frickin' club. The only decent thing to do with Cluetrain is to bury the sucker now while there's still time, before it begins to smell of management philosophy. Invite the neighbours over, hold a wake. Throw a wild and drunken orgy of a party. Because only death is static. Life moves on.

How do you speak in a human voice? First, you get a life. And corporations just can't do that. Corporations are like Pinocchio. Or Frankenstein. Their noses grow longer at the oddest moments, or they start breaking things for no good reason. They want to be human, but gosh, they're not. They want the Formula for Life – but they want it so they can institutionalise it. The problem, of course, is that life is anti-formulaic, anti-institutional. The most fundamental quality of life is something the corporation can never capture, never possess. Life can't be shrink-wrapped, caged, dissected, analysed or owned. Life is free.

And so, finally, the question we've all been waiting for. In the newly humanised and highly vocal global marketplace the Internet has helped create, can corporations survive at all? Not if they're unable to speak for themselves. Not if they're literally dumbfounded by the changes taking place all around them.

But maybe – and it's a big maybe – companies can get out of their own way. Maybe they can become much looser associations of free individuals. Maybe they can cut 'their' people enough slack to actually act and sound like people instead of 1950s science-fiction robots. Gort need more sales! Gort need make quota! You not buy now, Gort nuke your planet!

Easy there, Gort. Calm down boy. Here, chew on this kryptonite.

Everybody's laughing. No one gives a rat's ass. So here's another question. Perhaps you even thought of it yourself. How come this book ended up in the business section of your local bookstore instead of under Humour, Horror or True Crime? Hey, don't look at us.

Fact is, we don't care about business – per se, per diem, au gratin. Given half a chance, we'd burn the whole constellation of obsolete business concepts to the waterline. Cost of sales and bottom lines and profit margins – if you're a company, that's your problem. But if you *think* of yourself as a company, you've got much bigger worries. We strongly suggest you repeat the following mantra as often as possible until you feel better: 'I am not a company. I am a human being.'

So, no, at the end of all this we don't have a cogent set of recommendations. We don't have a crystal ball we can use to help business plot its future course. We don't have any magic-bullet cure for Corporate Linguistic Deficit Disorder. Did that much come across? OK, just checking.

However, we do have a vision of what life could be like if we ever make it through the current transition. It's hard for some to imagine the Era of Total Cluelessness coming to a close. But try. Try hard. Because only imagination can finally bring the curtain down.

Imagine a world where everyone was constantly learning, a world where what you wondered was more interesting than what you knew, and curiosity counted for more than certain knowledge. Imagine a world where what you gave away was more valuable than what you held back, where joy was not a dirty word, where play was not forbidden after your 11th birthday. Imagine a world in which the business of business was to imagine worlds people might actually want to live in someday. Imagine a world created by the people, for the people not perishing from the earth forever.

Yeah. Imagine that.

ACKNOWLEDGEMENTS

THIS BOOK IS THE RESULT of literally thousands of conversations over the course of many years with friends, colleagues, online acquaintances, readers of our various 'zines, and the signatories of *The Cluetrain Manifesto*. While we are grateful to all, it would be impossible to thank everyone individually. However, we owe a particular debt of gratitude to the following people who made especially generous direct contributions to the project:

Tom Petzinger, Jr of *The Wall Street Journal*, an early *Cluetrain* enthusiast and the author of the best business book of the past five years.

Dan Gillmor, who despite strong reservations about *The Manifesto's* style deemed it significant enough to cover it in the *San Jose Mercury News*.

Bob Gahl, Dan Pritchett, and the team at The Sphere Information Services **(www.thesphere.net)** for hosting cluetrain.com.

Jacqueline Murphy, our unflappable editor at Perseus.

Dinah 'Metagrrl' Sanders, who pitched in to help create and maintain the Cluetrain Web site.

Susan, David, Sarah and Naomi Levine for letting the authors invade their aerie for our face-to-face meetings.

And we give a very warm acknowledgement to David Miller of The Garamond Agency, the 'fifth engineer' who understood instantly what we were on about, and pulled us through the entire process with insight, friendship and warmth. Thanks, David!

ABOUT THE AUTHORS

Rick Levine

(rick.levine@levinesquared.com)

I ESCAPED FROM THE film and video world 20 years ago to do CBT authoring system design for Control Data's PLATO group. Later, I was one of the first software people in the door at Sun Microsystems' East Coast Division, and managed software for the industry's first Intel-based UNIX workstation.

At Sun, I specialised in user-interface design and development, product usability and, in the last several years, wrapping businesses around the Web. Among my 'firsts' at Sun were the creation of Sun's first usability testing laboratory, the first integration of visual design disciplines into Sun's software development process, the design of the industry's first 'magazine' Web site layout and the creation of the first Web applications with two-way integration of data between internal company databases and Sun's external Web presence.

My recent accomplishments include the conception and creation of the Java Developer Connection, a Web site resource for Java technologists, with more than 1 000 000 members in 130 countries. I'm a founder of the Information and Content Exchange (ICE) protocol authoring group, an innovative Internet protocol for the syndication and distribution of Web content, and I'm co-author of the W3C note specifying the ICE protocol. I've been granted patents on computer-based help systems, Web-based shopping cart technology and Web navigation techniques.

Along the way, my brother Neil and I created **www.hatfactory.com**, a neat little commerce site to sell hats.

As this book is going to print, I'm starting a job as co-founder and CTO of a Boulder e-commerce start-up at **www.mancala.com**.

I'd like to thank Sue and the kids for putting up with my bringing a laptop to Kauai to finish this book, and Neil for not running the other way whenever I phone with 'another small graphics job'.

Christopher Locke

(clocke@panix.com)

THROUGH A COMBINATION of dumb luck and happy accident, I've managed to work with some very interesting technologies: artificial intelligence in Japan in the early eighties, robotics at Carnegie Mellon University at the turn of the decade, then CAD-CAM, concurrent engineering, and SGML in the early nineties. I was an early and vocal proponent of open commercial use of the Internet, once reserved exclusively to the military-industrial-academic complex. In 1994, I launched one of the first Web-based e-commerce systems through relationships I forged with Digital Equipment, EDS, Ogilvy & Mather, Dun & Bradstreet, Anderson Consulting, and several dozen other firms. I later worked on Internet initiatives at IBM and MCI. Today, I run a Web consulting practice in Boulder, Colorado, plus I write and speak about the sorts of ideas you've been reading here.

I would like to thank my wife, Lauren, for putting up with book writing and much else, plus my fabulously bright and sparky nine-year-old daughter, Selene, who now calls my computer Monitor Lewinsky. Special thanks are due to Tom Stewart at Fortune for many conversations about industrial history, and to Steve Larsen, good friend and EVP-Marketing at Net Perceptions – when the book was down to deadline, he carefully overlooked my delays in bringing **personalization.com** online. I'd also like to thank the readers of my e-zine, *Entropy Gradient Reversals*, for invaluable feedback, feedforward and the willing suspension of disbelief that has enabled me to push the boundaries of my writing beyond the limits of community decency and common sense. Finally, I have to thank my evil twin and alter ego,

RageBoy, for destroying the last vestiges of my sanity several years ago, thus opening the way to everything I've been able to accomplish since.

http://www.panix.com/~clocke
http://www.rageboy.com

Doc Searls

(doc@searls.com)

NOT LONG AFTER I MET JOYCE – the patient, brilliant and beautiful woman who would later become my wife – she asked for a full accounting of all my prior career moves: ice cream truck driver; wholesale produce grunt; newspaper and magazine photographer and editor; social programme bureaucrat; radio salesman, engineer and air personality; advertising agency co-founder and creative director, PR agency chief, marketing consultant – and several other identities I had repressed up to that point.

She homed in on radio. Why did I leave it? When? I don't remember my answers, but I do remember her response. 'That's when you sold out,' she said. Suddenly it seemed significant that my nickname, Doc, is the eroded remnant of Doctor Dave, which was the name I used on the air.

Everything I've done since radio has been in advertising, PR and marketing. And I've done well at all three. For a few years our agency, Hodskins Simone & Searls, was very hot stuff in Silicon Valley. My own clients have included Apple, Inprise (formerly Borland), Logitech, Pretty Good Privacy, Novell, Symantec, Hitachi, Motorola, and many more. And over the same period my writing has appeared in *OMNI*, *PC Magazine*, *Upside* and *The Globe and Mail*, among other publications, including my own Web 'zine, Reality 2.0.

But nothing felt like radio again – until *Cluetrain*. Here, finally, I got to rant and joke and speak Truth like I hadn't done in 25 years. It's been a blast. My first thanks go to Joyce, for both inspiring and putting up with me. Also to our three-year-old son,

Jeffrey, who did the same. And finally to my new employer, *Linux Journal*, for lending me the time it took to commit the acts of arson in this book.

David Weinberger

(**self@evident.com**)

I HATE WRITING ABOUT MYSELF. So, here's some minimalist context.

I taught philosophy for six years at a couple of colleges. Loved my students, felt uncomfortable with my peers. I simultaneously had been writing for a wide variety of magazines, specialising in humour and technology. My writing experience let me move into marketing (thus flipping my philosophical values on their head). Over the years I've worked as a 'strategic marketing' person inside and outside various high tech companies, some small, some big. I've had the good luck to work with very smart people and businesses from the earliest days of the Web and learned a lot.

I spend about half my time consulting and the other half writing and speaking about the Web's effect on how we work and live together. I write columns for some magazines, am a commentator on National Public Radio's 'All Things Considered', and publish my own free 'zine, JOHO (**www.hyperorg.com**). You can reach me at **self@evident.com**.

I owe thanks to Open Text (a former employer) for letting me use their trademarked phrase, 'The Hyperlinked Organization', and for setting the four of us up with Livelink, their Web-based collaborative work management system.

I owe an especial thanks to the subscribers to *JOHO* for engaging me in conversations from which I've learned so much. They are a smart and very funny (ha-ha and peculiar) bunch.

Most of all, to my family for putting up with me while I was working on this book: Thank you Ann, Jennie, Leah and Nathan. I love you.